Call of The Divine

Kathy McCutcheon

Dedication

This is dedicated to the Divine. You have watched over me and protected me my entire life, through every lifetime. You inspired this book when I began my healing Spiritual Awakening Journey. You have brought me so far and shown me that the only way to you is to heal the Inner Child.

Thank you, Almighty Father, for your love, protection, guidance, and most of all, for those loving messages you give and those quiet conversations we share each day. Being in your presence moves my Soul so much that I am overwhelmed with emotion. I love you, and I pray this brings your children home to you, as is the desire of your heart!

Acknowledgment

I want to acknowledge all who chose to negatively affect me throughout my lifetime. I thank you for allowing the Divine to work through you to refine me into my authentic self. The pain inflicted and the things I was burdened with or wrongfully taken from me have only strengthened me for the final battle of my final existence. And look! I did it! I completed my Karmic cycle and have broken generational curses, freeing ancestors and past loved ones from millennia of bondage!

So, thank you for making me the warrior and winner I am today!

I am free!

I am beautiful!

I am worthy!

I AM DIVINE!

About the Author

Kathleen McCutcheon is 61 years of age. Her chosen career was in the legal field as a legal secretary, but she has recently retired. Born in Indiana, she currently resides in Oklahoma.

Since embarking on her Spiritual Awakening Journey, she has begun to renew and rediscover hobbies and interests that were previously lost to her. She enjoys taking nature walks, thrifting, meditating, and tending to her house plants. She is absolutely sure that she will discover more as she allows her Inner Child to expand and explore the wonders and magic of the Divine world!

Call of The Divine

Standing on the back steps, I banged on the screen door, desperately needing to get in. I had to use the bathroom and knew failing to reach it in time would lead to an accident, and then I would be punished for it.

"Mommy, mommy, please let me in. I have to go potty!!"

Tears streamed down my face as I tugged on the handle, but it wouldn't budge. I yelled for her again, but there was no response.

The temperature rose, causing sweat to form on my forehead and above my lip, the sun beating down on me.

"Mommy, please open the door!"

Even at three years old, I understood the severe consequences of soiling myself. Clearly, potty training was not progressing well.

I couldn't hold it any longer, fear tightening around my heart, adrenaline coursing through my veins. I heard her footsteps on the stairs, then across the kitchen floor. My breathing grew labored, and my tears flowed even more freely.

"What the hell is wrong with you?"

"I need to potty."

"Come here!"

She yanked me by my arm, realized I had soiled myself and berated and struck me while cleaning me up. Then, she placed me on the toilet as punishment.

Years later, I realized my interruptions were during moments between her and my father, marking me as an extreme inconvenience.

This is the first memory I have of my mother. I want to say that this is the only instance of such a thing happening to me, but unfortunately, it wasn't.

This incident, among others, confirmed to me that I had always been seen as a bother, even before my birth.

Contents

Chapter 1: Echoes of Innocence Lost

"I cried out to God for help; I cried out to God to hear me. When I was in distress, I sought the Lord; at night I stretched out untiring hands, and I would not be comforted."
—Psalm 77, Verse 1 and 2

My first memory of my mother is one filled with cruelty, abuse, hate, and a lack of love. This treatment never improved as I grew from a child into an adolescent and then a young adult. Her negative feelings towards me seemed to intensify with each life challenge I faced. I suspect her resentment and disdain for me began even before my birth.

I grew up hearing that my father had impregnated another woman at the same time my mother was carrying me. This means I might have a half-sibling out there. Interestingly, my oldest sister took an ancestry test, like I did, probably hoping to find this other sibling.

My father was due to be stationed in California. Instead of taking my mother and the three oldest kids, he chose to go with the other woman. He sent my mother and the children back to Indiana to stay with her parents. This situation coincided with her being pregnant with me. The details are fuzzy, but this is what I've been told.

I've always been the anomaly in our family of five children—the odd one out. I'm the only one born in September and the only one born in Indiana, our parents' home state. My siblings each hold a distinct place in our family: the oldest girl is celebrated for being the firstborn, the second for being the only boy, and the third for being the middle child. Then comes me, and after me, finally comes the youngest girl, cherished for being the baby. Amidst them, I felt like an afterthought, a sore thumb sticking out, which only served as another reason for differential treatment.

The story goes that I wasn't planned for. My mother supposedly marked a safe day on the calendar incorrectly, and my father chose not to attend church that Sunday. To my mother, I was a mistake from the start. She never spoke negatively about my siblings like that.

The only positive stories she shared involved their births, like one being born during a blizzard, which could have been my brother in New York or my youngest sister in Illinois. My other sisters were born in California and Texas. These stories are the only ones I recall her sharing about the birth of her children.

I don't recall seeing my mother hit my siblings as much as she hit me. Perhaps it's because I didn't share their experiences. My own interactions with her were uniquely affected by her relationship with her husband — a man not present in my siblings' early lives as much as he was in mine. This aspect of our relationship, and the denial of it by my siblings, seems to distort their memories of him.

He entered our lives when I was two, by which time my older siblings were well on their way to adolescence — six, eight, and twelve years old. The gaps between our ages matched the intervals of my father's deployments, as he was frequently away for two to four years due to his military commitments.

It's clear that his presence and absence were closely tied to his military orders. I assume some portions of his career were spent stateside, with his family nearby, though I was too young to remember or have solid evidence. The timing of our births might align more with his stints abroad than with the effectiveness of the natural family planning method endorsed by the Catholic Church, which suggests avoiding intercourse seven days before and after ovulation.

My grandfather ran a small dairy farm. If memory serves, he had around twenty dairy cows. After milking, I remember visiting the small building where he pasteurized the milk before it was collected in large silver containers by a man with a pickup truck.

My grandfather, or "Papaw" as I called him, would always bring a bucket of milk to my grandmother for the fridge. Visiting home was something I cherished. After the passing of my father's mother and then my mother's father (Papaw), I returned only twice. Once, when my mother went on a trip with an admirer for whom she had little affection, she left my sister and me with our grandmother. The other visit occurred in my twenties when my grandmother was ill.

When I was young, we returned to our hometown a couple of times. I always looked forward to these visits as they were the best moments of my early childhood. The journey there seemed endless, yet the trip back felt much shorter. Although we visited my father's parents, I preferred the time spent at my Papaw's house. The visits with my father's family were, to put it mildly, dull.

My paternal grandfather, confined to his bedroom with an oxygen tank, barely interacted with us other than to offer peppermints I didn't like. His room was always dark, and his thin, bony appearance frightened me. I was about five years old when he died from liver disease caused by alcoholism. My grandmother wasn't very familiar with us but clearly adored my father, treating him as if he could do no wrong.

Since none of my father's siblings had children my age, I felt isolated and eager to return to Papaw's house. I had many cousins to play with there, making it the place I considered "home."

During a visit, Papaw had a young and pregnant heifer for the first time. She held a special place in his heart. When it was time for the evening milking, she didn't come in with the rest of the herd, and night was falling. Papaw suspected she was giving birth somewhere and struggling, so I accompanied him to check on her, hoping to prevent any coyote attacks if she was in the woods.

We found her at the far end of the pasture, in the midst of labor and facing complications. Papaw quickly assessed the situation. The calf was positioned incorrectly, but with experience and calm, he assisted the heifer, successfully delivering the calf. Witnessing this, I was filled with admiration for Papaw. For a city kid like me, this was an extraordinary moment. The birth of a calf was mesmerizing on its own, but seeing Papaw's skillful intervention was awe-inspiring. I was around eight years old then, and the experience left a lasting impression on me. Papaw was already my hero, but his actions that day elevated him to an almost mythical status in my eyes. To this day, I hold no one in higher regard. Even after his passing, I feel his guidance to this very day. It feels like he's still watching over me, paralleling the protective love of the Divine. It's a constant reminder of the ever-present support and calling from the Divine to my Higher Self.

Papaw had built a modest house where they lived; it was the birthplace of eight of my grandparents' nine children. The ninth child, the only one born in a hospital and bottle-fed, died as an infant due to a heart condition. My mother would recount how Papaw believed the hospital birth and bottle-feeding were to blame.

The house had a large room directly accessible from the enclosed porch, a kitchen more akin to a small bedroom, and an actual bedroom. Upstairs was a single large room that spanned the entire first floor. I remember my mother and her younger sister sharing stories about their childhood hardships, including how my mother often had to sacrifice her own needs for her siblings.

A particularly poignant story from my mother's childhood centered around Christmas. Each girl received a porcelain doll, but when tasked with fetching them, my mother accidentally dropped hers on the wooden stairs, causing it to shatter. Her parents' response was unsympathetic; she was told it was her fault for trying to carry them all and that she would have to go without hers.

These experiences seemingly shaped my mother into the person she became, marked by bitterness. She and her father were very close until her younger sister's birth, which made my mother no longer the youngest, sparking jealousy. This jealousy extended into her adult relationships, particularly with men who showed attention to other women.

In an act of bravado, my mother made a bet with one of her sisters that she could perform a somersault while she was nine months pregnant with me. Despite the risk to my safety, including the potential of the umbilical cord wrapping around my neck, she went through with it.

I was born with a "blister" on my head, attributed to lying incorrectly against the pelvic bone. My grandfather showed me extra concern and attention because of this. I grew up believing this story, which might explain a small bald spot on the left side of my head, possibly the result of that somersault.

My mother recounted how my grandfather encouraged her to bring me to the barn for the morning and evening milking sessions. They would place me in the manager, and he would keep an eye on me while he worked. This experience, returning to her father's home with her children, may have ignited feelings of resentment and jealousy in her.

Once the cherished daughter, she likely expected to reclaim her special status, especially with her younger sister and other siblings no longer at home. She imagined it would be her chance to have her father's undivided attention. However, instead of receiving the sympathy she anticipated for being sent away by her husband, she found herself sharing her father's attention with me, which resurrected old feelings of jealousy and bitterness that she had harbored against her siblings.

This situation was further complicated because, in her eyes, not only had her husband rejected her because of me, but I had also usurped her position with her father. The result was a transfer of her pent-up anger, resentment, and hatred onto me, manifesting in various forms of abuse once we left her father's house. She felt justified in her actions, seeing me as her property, to be treated however she saw fit without intervention.

Her temper was unpredictable and could be triggered by any perceived slight or error, especially if it related to something my father did or didn't do. A minor mistake on such a day meant trouble was imminent.

I vividly remember how everyone would scatter to avoid her wrath when she was "on the warpath," a phrase she used to signal her foul mood. On good weather days, we knew to stay outside until dinner time, signaled by the streetlight at the block's end.

In bad weather, the strategy was to stay off her radar, retreat to our rooms, and keep as quiet as possible. The only exception was the youngest sibling, who was always spared from her ire.

My earliest memory is of Papaw lifting me onto my pony, Whiskers, a gift he had chosen for me. I remember hearing that Whiskers was either partially or completely blind. I was just nine months old at the time. Papaw placed me on Whiskers and led us onto the house's enclosed porch.

My joy quickly turned to displeasure when he placed one of my cousins behind me on my pony. Even as a young child, I fiercely felt that Whiskers was mine.

"NO! THIS IS MY PONY! GET OFF!"

The words echo in my memory, alongside the vivid sensation of jealousy and my small hand pushing against my cousin, urging them to get off.

It wasn't until my adult years that my mother showed me pictures from that day, revealing I was only nine months old at the time.

The clarity of that memory astounds me. It is as vivid as if it happened yesterday. I believe this memory has lingered to ensure my earliest life recollection is one of happiness, joy, and unconditional love from the one person who truly loved me.

On that day, I don't remember any interactions with my parents, only the warmth of my grandfather's embrace and the joy and smiles on our faces. It remains the most cherished memory of my life. Regardless of how much time passes, that day is as clear in my mind as if it were this morning.

Chapter 2: Shadows of a Fractured Home

The story of my life continued. I have a lot of memories from my childhood, some good, most of them not so good. Yet, as I think back to them, they remind me of the hardships I have been through and the guidance and protection I received from the Divine. I am always grateful for that.

Our next home was in Paxton, Illinois. I have only a few memories of living there. One early memory is of my mother scolding me as I peeked into my sister's playpen. I was warned about the risk of tipping it over.

I remember chasing my older sister around the house. This woke up my father. As he descended the stairs, I tried to hide. He caught me and spanked me mid-air. My sisters, sitting quietly on the couch, were not punished. That was the only time my father ever spanked me. He made sure I learned my lesson. From then on, I had a deep-seated fear of him.

My father was a tall man, six feet tall and weighing about two hundred ten pounds. As a small child, aged two to six, I barely reached his waist. Now that I am five feet three inches tall, I remember how intimidating he was. To me, he was like a tall, sturdy oak tree, unbreakable and immovable.

I vaguely remember lying on my back on the kitchen table. I was in my Halloween costume. My mother was giving me an enema, insisting I couldn't go trick-or-treating until I had gone to the bathroom. Everyone was waiting for me. I was crying, upset at the thought of missing trick-or-treating. This experience made me less fond of Halloween.

As a result, I didn't enjoy dressing up my children for trick-or-treating. We didn't do it much after moving to Oklahoma. When my children were of age, concerns about candy tampering made me reluctant to take them out in the neighborhood.

I remember a moment with a woman and a small girl, around kindergarten age - that girl was me. I was dressed in a green dress, a white cardigan, and black patent leather shoes with side buckles. We were laid down for a nap in what seemed to me like a huge bed. That's all I can recall from that time. I guess it was after kindergarten, and I was there while my mother was at work, waiting for her to pick me up.

I also recall a bike ride with my brother and older sister to a candy store, which we weren't supposed to do. During the ride, my younger sister's foot got caught in the bike's spokes, injuring her. We all faced the consequences of that adventure.

Another memory involves my older sister walking home in the snow, leading to frostbite on her feet. My mother was furious, blaming a teacher for sending her home inadequately dressed. My sister struggled with foot problems for the rest of her life.

I can recall my older sister sucking her thumb until she was fourteen. To me, that signified some level of emotional and mental distress.

Once, while watching my brother's baseball game, a fly ball flew over the fence and hit me in the eye. I was about four years old. My mother was a huge baseball fan, particularly of the Chicago Cubs. I think her affection for the Cubs stemmed from our proximity to Chicago, as we lived in Paxton, Illinois, and my younger sister was born there. I remember what seemed like a massive cathedral, a Roman Catholic Church, where I believe we attended Sunday Mass. It was conducted in a language unfamiliar to me, which I later understood to be Latin. In the 1960s, the Catholic Church held Mass in Latin, the original language of the Church based in Rome, Italy.

I recall standing beside my father, who seemed as tall as an oak tree to me, and hearing the powerful sound of the organ and choir. I sang along as well as I could, not fully grasping it then but feeling deeply moved. I was no older than five.

Since a young age, I've felt a connection to what I refer to as the Divine, a calling that felt like it claimed my Soul and heart. I believe this connection has spanned my past lives into this one, maintaining my dedication to the Divine. The commitments I made in past lifetimes, whether as a nun, monk, or high priestess, are still honored by my Higher Self today. However, it took me time to realize I was a creator like the Divine, capable of magical creation.

My abilities to see spirits, read Tarot, and receive messages from the Divine and the Ancestors were always with me, though not always recognized. Whenever I shared these visions with my mother, the person I trusted most, she dismissed them as imagination or dreams, urging me to stop making things up. Consequently, I began to ignore these experiences, and they faded away until recently.

My bond with the Divine has been a constant in my life, even when I was unaware of it. I've always had what some might call a Christ consciousness. Throughout my life, I've found myself praying for things that, according to the Divine, I didn't need or wouldn't receive. Yet, I was still responding to the call from my Higher Self to connect with the Divine. It just took me longer to embark on my Spiritual Awakening Journey.

I recall picking rhubarb from our backyard. My mother used it in meals, but I'm unsure if she made pie or simply boiled it as a side dish. It grew wild around our home, surrounded by a long gravel driveway but no fences, stretching from the front to an alley at the back.

One night, I saw an old hobo rummaging through our garbage cans from an upstairs window. That sight really scared me, and I always disliked the dark alley, fearing what might hide in the shadows.

I also remember watching "Dark Shadows" with my mother. It was a soap opera from the '60s and early '70s featuring werewolves and vampires. Quinton was the werewolf character, and my mother adored "Quinton's Theme," his associated melody.

One afternoon, during a particularly scary scene, I suddenly realized I was sitting alone. Everyone else had vanished. To this day, I wonder if they left me there on purpose. It felt like just one of the many times my siblings picked on me and, yes, even my mother.

Thinking back, it's baffling why anyone would let a four- or five-year-old watch such a show. This choice came back to haunt her when we attended my paternal grandfather's funeral. Following Catholic tradition, we were supposed to kiss the deceased goodbye.

As my mother lifted me, I noticed my grandfather's eyelid twitch. Innocently, I asked if he would come back as a vampire. The room went silent, and everyone's attention suddenly fell on us. My mother, embarrassed, quickly pulled me away, gripping my arm so tightly I nearly fell.

I didn't understand what I had said wrong. To me, coming back from the dead, like on the show, was a genuine concern. It was my first encounter with death; how was I to know any different? My mother's reaction drew even more attention, and she hurried me out of the room. I don't remember if I was punished for my question, but she made sure I knew it was inappropriate.

My father cherished Cadillacs, viewing them as a symbol of status or celebrity. We always had one. He kept a Cadillac on blocks in our shed/garage, located at the back of our yard near the alley. Unfortunately, a fire broke out there, destroying his prized possession. I was too young to recall the incident's specifics or what caused the fire, but I know it deeply upset him for many years, even before Alzheimer's affected his memory.

Afterward, my family moved to Oklahoma. By then, I was six and starting first grade. We lived on Silver meadow Drive. The layout of that house is still clear in my mind, though I'm not sure why.

I have a distinct memory of one Easter morning. My mother was ironing while my little sister and I, having just woken up, came into the living room to find our Easter baskets. That's all I remember about that day, and I'm not sure why it stands out to me.

Perhaps something significant happened that I've since blocked out. Another memory involves me being found by my mother asleep in my wagon in the garage. I don't recall how I got there. She woke me, puzzled at my presence in the garage, and I had no explanation, leading me to think I might have been sleepwalking.

My father owned several five-gallon glass pickle jars filled with Cracker Jack toys, which we were strictly forbidden to touch. Yet, my mother discovered one jar in the wagon with me, its lid removed. I've always wondered about that since those jars were stored on the highest shelf, well beyond my reach as a child.

A lingering question from my childhood concerns how I contracted cold sores, a form of herpes. I ponder how a young child could come into contact with an STD. It suggests I must have been exposed by an adult, as there's no way I could have acquired it on my own at six years old.

In the family, I am the only child who experienced it. Every year, around the end of September or early October, I would always have an outbreak during picture day at school, and they would always be in the photos. That seems odd to me, especially in light of my father's dubious past.

He had several ladies while serving abroad. He was definitely molesting children while he was stationed in Asian nations, in my opinion. It stands to reason that if you are willing to transgress boundaries with your daughter, you would be equally willing to do so with other kids. It goes without saying that those nations have a long history of child trafficking; as a result, I'm sure my father was sating his pedophilic desires in addition to frequenting brothels and other establishments. There is no doubt, in my opinion, that he was infected with STDs. I spent my first-grade year at Cleveland Bailey Elementary School. During recess, I experienced having one of my fingers crushed, resulting in the loss of a fingernail. I also remember a small yard light, resembling a streetlamp, placed at the corner of the sidewalk that led from our driveway to the house.

Our house, which lacked a fence in the backyard, faced a field that stretched for a mile and a half behind it. While we lived there, my father worked at a couple of places. He drove a delivery truck for Borden Milk, an old brand, and had another job before he started working at TAFB. These are my limited memories from that time; we didn't stay there long.

The following year, my family moved into a house they had purchased. It featured three bedrooms, one and three-quarter bathrooms, a den, a fireplace, a two-car garage, and an in-ground pool. In the early '70s, having an in-ground pool was quite luxurious.

The house was on Ridgewood Drive, in one of the town's upper-middle-class neighborhoods. Being seven at the time, I was thrilled about having our own pool. To us kids, it was the highlight of the new home.

During this period, I completed my First Communion, a significant rite in the Catholic faith. This ceremony marks the first time a person receives the sacrament of Communion, symbolizing the eating of Jesus Christ's Body and drinking His Blood. Participants consume an unleavened wafer, representing the Body of Christ, and grape juice, signifying His Blood, both of which have been blessed by the priest. For this occasion, seven-year-old girls are dressed to resemble miniature brides, adorned in white dresses, veils, gloves, lace ankle socks, and patent leather shoes, and each carries a miniature Bible. Part of the ritual involves memorizing and reciting a Bible verse to the priest before partaking in the Body and Blood of Christ.

As I recall from the 1960s, this practice was a deeply entrenched tradition. There was even an 8mm film capturing the event, strangely sharing a reel with footage from a family swimming party. My desire to excel in the ceremony was driven by a longing to make my mother proud, seeking her approval and validation.

In second grade, I attended Ridgecrest Elementary. That year, I remember a girl who had an extensive collection of crayons in a large, transparent zip bag. She refused to share them and later became one of my bullies through junior high and high school.

Interestingly, our daughters became best friends in junior high and remained so for thirty years until a significant disagreement ended their friendship.

The girl's mother harbored a longstanding grudge against me from our school days, affecting our potential friendship despite my efforts to reconcile for the sake of our daughters. Her animosity seemed unfounded, perhaps rooted in jealousy, a sentiment that eventually mirrored in the fallout between our daughters. There were two boys in my class, Rex and Arthur, whose last names escaped me. Arthur stands out in my memory. At eight years old and having been held back a year, he caught my young heart with his dark hair and eyes. Early in the school year, they came to my house, tossing pennies at me from across the street before riding away on their bikes.

I faintly recall a game of Spin the Bottle at my house, where I got to kiss Arthur. I was overjoyed. Arthur's sister, a classmate of mine, had a best friend who also fancied Arthur and was jealous of my interaction with him.

Unbeknownst to me, these girls befriended me to drive a wedge between Arthur and me, leading to trouble that caused him to stop speaking to me. I remember praying and wishing for Arthur to like me. When it seemed my dream had come true, it was quickly snatched away, setting a recurring theme in my life: coming close to achieving my desires only to have them slip away or be taken from me at the last moment.

Mean girls plagued my childhood and followed me into adulthood. My mother's behavior had stripped me of any fight. I would cower in anticipation of her reach, similar to a dog fearing a hit from its owner.

This fear arose whether she was angered by something I did, if I failed to prevent my younger sibling from mischief, or if a chore was left incomplete despite my efforts elsewhere. Her short temper made it essential to learn all the tasks and always stay alert quickly.

Her temper made me hypersensitive.

I was constantly tuned in not just to my own senses but to those of everyone around me, to my environment, and to the needs, wants, and desires of others. I felt compelled to ensure everything was done correctly, including tasks she hadn't assigned. This expectation to maintain a pristine environment under threat of consequences deeply affected me. No wonder I became a people pleaser, always anxious and nervous.

I went to St. Philip Neri Catholic School from third to fifth grade. My relationship with my mother and the limited memories I have from these school days disturbed me more than anything else.

Given how abusive my mother could be, I'm amazed she wasn't raised Catholic. It appeared as though she had attended a nuns' "Guilt and Shame 101" course. Tuesdays in Classroom 3A at 10:00 a.m. with Sister Anne. "Spare the Rod Spoil the Child 201 " with Sister Mary in the gymnasium on Mondays and Wednesdays at 3:00 and 7:00 p.m.

I think my father's issues originated from there. I also believe that his training as an altar boy made him accustomed to all this, and he later used that training to train his own victims. His younger sisters were his first victims, then young girls abroad, victims of his overseas deployments, and then his own girls came next.

This "disease" was inherited by his oldest grandson from his son. Reports about his grandson's inappropriate behavior with both male and female family members exist, but nobody wants to acknowledge the reality. There is the impregnation of a first cousin, the abortion of the subsequent child, and the molestation of both male and female cousins.

Oh, the secrets we hold onto and the facts we hide, reject, and decide to ignore because we believe that if we do, they will magically disappear!

During those three years, my memories are scarce. I recall participating in a volleyball tournament and playing the clarinet in the school band. It wasn't a marching band, just an elective class. I enjoyed making music, though I never mastered reading it. I relied on my ability to play by ear, memorizing songs to replicate them.

My fifth-grade teacher, Ms. Cynthia Peel, stands out vividly in my memory. She had freckles, red hair, and a noticeable disability that caused her to walk with a significant limp due to a misshapen right hip. Her demeanor often seemed harsh, as if she resented her condition and projected that frustration onto others.

As a child, I was incredibly nervous and anxious, likely a result of my home life and how my mother treated me. This stress manifested physically as severe psoriasis on my scalp. To treat it, my mother used a sulfuric acid shampoo prescribed by a doctor, leaving a rotten egg smell. She also applied castor oil to my scalp to keep it from flaking and scabbing, which made my hair look greasy and dirty. I felt deeply embarrassed by my appearance and tried to draw as little attention to myself as possible.

One day, while assisting a classmate with spelling, Ms. Peel and I had a disagreement about why I was out of my seat and talking. She sent me to the hallway for being disruptive. Upon returning to class, she humiliated me in front of everyone by saying, "Do not return to my class until you have washed your hair."

This incident left me in tears, overwhelmed with embarrassment and shame. I went home and shared the ordeal with my mother.

My mother had a rule: she could say or do anything to her children, but no one else could. She had stormed the school once before when a nun punished my older sister by making her stand in a trash can, calling her "white trash."

My mother's temper was fierce, and she did not take this lightly. She had previously confronted a nun and priest over my sister's treatment, and this situation with Ms. Peel was shaping up to be no different. After my mother dealt with Ms. Peel, the principal, Sister Alice, and the church's priest, Ms. Peel was left in tears. I'm not sure if she came back to finish the semester or even returned the next year.

Sister Alice and the priest were somewhat prepared for my mother's wrath, having encountered her the previous year. Still, they were not happy with the encounter. My mother had certainly made a name for herself as someone who did not tread lightly with the church staff or possibly even the congregation.

After that incident, I disengaged emotionally. If Ms. Peel had come back to teach, she would have been undoubtedly more cautious around me for the rest of the year. Sadly, my mother did not show the same determination to protect me from a pedophile who caused me emotional and mental harm.

Her judgment on what constituted a threat to her children was questionable at best. She often seemed confused and placed my needs last. My well-being was always secondary to her desires and those of others around her, including her other children. There was a time when my parents were out together, a rare occurrence. My oldest sister, supposed to be in charge, had stepped out. My baby sister became upset with me for not helping her look for a missing shoe.

While I was lying on my back on the bed, she threw a vinyl record album at me. It struck me right between the eyes, causing blood to spurt like a fountain, even lifting the comic book off my face.

The bleeding was relentless, spurting with every heartbeat for two hours and soaking through four bath towels. It would briefly stop, only to resume when my sister checked on it. I'm amazed I didn't bleed to death. Upon their return, my parents were surprisingly indifferent, not bothering with a hospital visit or a doctor the next day. My little sister faced no repercussions. Had our roles been reversed, I would have been severely punished. The incident left me with a one-inch scar.

My memories also include sharing birthdays (though I was the only one who shared), clothes, shoes—practically everything. Except for the baby, she shared nothing. Using anything of hers, even if she wasn't using it, was off-limits and would cause an uproar.

We shared a room and were supposed to share the chore of cleaning it to our mother's standards. Inevitably, I ended up cleaning my sister's mess because she wouldn't. To this day, she struggles with basic tasks. Her home is in disarray, resembling a hoarder's, with her life mirroring the chaos. All three of my sisters keep their homes in a state I find unacceptable. Their floors are dirty, dishes pile up in the sink, and clutter dominates every space. Shoes and other belongings are strewn everywhere, never in their proper place. This messiness baffles me because we were not raised in such an environment.

Saturday mornings in our childhood were dedicated to cleaning. Our mother maintained a spotless home and instilled those values in us. A clean, orderly environment is something I cherish; I cannot stand chaos. My slight OCD may be to blame, but it ensures my house is clean. While I wasn't as strict with my children, I did expect them to keep their rooms tidy.

I have dim recollections of visiting a couple's house for the Fourth of July, where we set off fireworks, and someone might have been injured, though I'm not certain. I remember outings to gather pecans and cut firewood. When I expressed to my father that trees have feelings, he dismissed it, but I've learned through a past life reading that I was once a fairy who cared for trees, confirming my beliefs.

One memorable outing was to Spring lake Amusement Park for my father's company picnic, shortly before he started working at TAFB in a civilian role.

I also remember watching "True Grit" at the Air Force Base theater with my parents. On the way home, I mimicked Groucho Marx with a bubble gum cigar, making my father laugh—one of the rare times I did so. The only other time was during a trip home from Indiana. Seeing pieces of a tire on the road, I joked, "Look, Dad, someone's tire is losing its skin."

It amused him greatly. These moments, when I was around eight or nine, are precious memories of the few times I brought laughter to my father.

I recall making only three or four trips to Indiana to visit my grandparents before my Papaw passed away. Among these visits, a few precious memories with Papaw stand out. I cherish the memory of a fishing trip, just the two of us, heading to a small pond with a bamboo pole and a few worms. My age at the time escapes me, but it's memories like these that I treasure deeply.

Another fond memory is being chosen to sit next to him in his pickup truck. A coffee can sat next to my leg on the truck's floor, serving as a spit can for his chewing tobacco. Sometimes, his spit would miss the can and hit my leg, but sitting next to my Papaw, I felt like I had the best seat in the house.

I also remember when my father let us pull back the rug in the den to slide on the wood floor in our socks, pretending to ice skate. We were probably inspired by watching the Olympics. The first Christmas after my father left, my little sister and I received a peculiar gift from my mother: one skate each.

Overjoyed at first, we quickly became upset and disappointed upon realizing each box contained only one skate. We believed her when she said she could only afford one skate for each of us, and we were in tears.

After all the gifts were opened and we cleaned up, she instructed us to check under the chair next to the tree. Hidden, there was a box with the other two skates we had asked for. These moments, spanning from when I was about seven to around fourteen, are rare but cherished memories.

During the summer leading into my seventh-grade year, a significant dream marked the beginning of a challenging period with my father. In the dream, he was driving with my little sister seated in the back. I leaned over the front seat as we drove down a two-lane highway. Police officers were rerouting traffic around an accident scene.

As I glanced outside, a shocking image met my eyes. My mother was lying face down in a pool of blood on the road, lifeless as if discarded. Disturbingly, my father drove past without acknowledging her presence. His face was devoid of any emotion, his gaze fixed forward, unresponsive to my frantic alerts about my mother being dead on the road.

Awoken by the dream, I rushed to my mother's room, only to find it empty. A quick search led me outside, where I found her, unharmed, standing at the driveway's end, waiting for her ride to work. After I shared the haunting dream with her, she managed to soothe my fears.

Reflecting on the dream, it seemed to foreshadow the emotional and mental distress my father's actions would inflict on my mother in the following years. Throughout this ordeal, I felt like a mere spectator, unable to influence the outcome.

My father remained singularly focused on his path, impervious to the fallout. This dream underscored my innate sense of discernment, hinting at my deep-rooted intuition. It was as if the Divine was attempting to brace my Higher Self for the impending turmoil, though I found myself unprepared for the eventual reality.

Furthermore, after my grandfather's passing in March 1975, he appeared to me in a moment that transcended a mere dream. Dressed in his characteristic white T-shirt and overalls, he sat in his black recliner at my bedside. This encounter felt intensely real; I even left my bed to sit beside him. He offered comforting words, urging me not to fear. While his visit was brief, his presence was profoundly reassuring.

I cherished his smile and the warmth of his hand, though I struggled to recall his exact words. They likely offered enlightenment or assurance of his protective watch over me. Perhaps it was also a caution about the forthcoming challenges with my father, with a promise of the Divine's protection—a promise that was faithfully kept.

I'm working to awaken the gifts I let become dormant, seeking to recover those lost memories. As they reemerge, the joy of trusting my instincts, my spirit team, and the Divine is unparalleled. It's a journey towards opening my Third Eye, leading me toward my purpose, allowing me to access hidden memories, connect with loved ones from the past, explore past lives, and glimpse the future.

Dark moments have also marked my journey. Many such memories are repressed, or I've dissociated them from my conscious mind. Yet, some are indelibly imprinted, unforgettable, and only forgivable as I strive to move forward. These are the experiences often dismissed by others, leading to victim blaming and shaming as if the wrongdoing were mine.

The betrayal deepened when I realized that the person I sought comfort and safety from had become my persecutor. My siblings, influenced by our mother, had been led to see me as dishonest. Despite confronting the one who wronged me and showing visible shame and guilt, my mother sided with him, accusing me of being the provocateur. It seems she either believed I was lying or viewed him as the victim, to the extent that she would welcome him back even now if he were still alive. You must understand this is a man who would take off his clothes in the kitchen, put them on "his chair," and walk through the house naked to his bedroom. And this wasn't the end of it. In the morning, he would get up and walk through the house to the kitchen and get dressed in the kitchen while drinking his morning coffee. This was all normal for him.

He would take a shower and walk around in a towel the rest of the evening with his penis and testicles hanging out. I can rarely ever remember him wearing clothes at home.

I had no idea that this was not normal. I learned of the situation's abnormality while visiting a friend. I was twelve and went to spend the night (for the first time) with a little girl down the street.

Looking back now, I can see why she and her mother looked at me like I was crazy when I asked why her father wore pajamas at home. I still wonder what they must have thought of it.

One night, my father had the entire family outside in the backyard after midnight, skinny dipping. We all went skinny dipping while he filmed it on 8mm film. Needless to say, my father was extremely inappropriate, and that's putting it mildly.

My older sister still has the film.

At one time, she wanted to put it on VHS tape and make copies for the entire family. Needless to say, I wasn't in favor of that idea at all. She's a bit strange and inappropriate herself, always over-sexualizing with everybody and everything.

She would even compare all things to it. If you want her to understand something, you have to compare or reference it in sexual terms; otherwise, good luck trying to explain things to her.

I do understand her problems and what she has been through; I know what she has been through. She is a Xanax popper - that is her escape from her bipolar, co-dependent, emotional, and mental trauma from the sexual encounters with our incestual father and the damage done from the years of stripping.

All of this is something that she does not see, or maybe she sees and does not want to acknowledge and address it.

It makes sense now why my mother never wanted anyone over at the house to play or to spend the night with us and why she did not want us to spend the night with anyone.

She was afraid people would find out about my father, which makes me believe she knew about his "problem" long before things started happening.

Chapter 3: Revelations in the Darkness

"And he said: 'Truly I tell you, unless you change and become like little children, you will never enter the kingdom of heaven… And whoever welcomes one such child in my name welcomes me. If anyone causes one of these little ones—those who believe in me—to stumble, it would be better for them to have a large millstone hung around their neck and to be drowned in the depths of the sea.'"
—Mathew Chapter 18, Verse 3 and 5-6

One time, my mother accused my father of having an affair with our neighbor down the street. My father was acquainted with the couple; the husband, I believe, worked with him or knew him through his job at the military base. They lived a few houses down from us.

The situation escalated a few weeks after my father visited their house during the day a couple of times at moments when the husband was absent. My mother became extremely upset, convinced that the neighbor's pregnancy was the result of an affair with my father. She vehemently accused him of infidelity, repeating her allegations not just to him but in our presence as well.

They had two children: a daughter, Deirdra, who was my age, and a son, Todd, who was about the same age as my little sister. We attended the same school, and an argument broke out between Deirdra and me after I echoed my mother's accusations about my father being the baby's father. The fallout was significant. I remember having to apologize to Deirdra and her family. It's likely my mother also received a stern reprimand, and there were undoubtedly consequences stemming from the incident. I don't recall the exact punishment from my parents, though I'm certain it involved physical discipline. My mother had a way of taking out her frustrations physically until she felt calmer. I probably faced severe consequences for spreading rumors that were unfounded, causing trouble for my mother with my father, and bringing shame upon her by voicing suspicions that highlighted her insecurities and embarrassed both of my parents. The root of the issue was her habit of making such remarks in our presence; I was merely repeating what I had been led to believe was true.

My father dismissed my mother as "crazy," a label many men resort to when their actions prompt such reactions from women. If they persistently engage in the same behaviors, rely on the same excuses, and exhibit narcissistic traits, they should anticipate similar responses and outcomes.

I am convinced that my father justified his unfaithfulness by blaming the characteristics or actions of my mother that supposedly drove him to it. Disregarding the fact that he was unfaithful while overseas, where she couldn't even exhibit the behaviors he likely accused her of when they were together at home. He misled her about needing to constantly know his whereabouts, even though he spent the majority of their marriage away from her, serving in the armed forces.

Any wife would yearn for her husband's company and that of his children upon his return to the States and after retiring, following an absence for over half their marriage. However, my mother's reaction was beyond the norm.

Indeed, my mother had her challenges. She is diagnosed with bipolar disorder and struggles with co-dependency, a pattern that seems to have passed down through generations. Additionally, she has a unique kind of fixation on my father – an ailment that, although not medically recognized or named, I believe is specific to her.

This condition appears to be unparalleled, as it requires being in her shoes with a partner like my father. It's an obsession that seems once in a lifetime, extremely unhealthy and repulsive to witness.

Her fixation with this man reached the extent that she deceived him into marrying her. At the age of twelve, she enlisted me to note down the mileage on his truck and to prepare his lunch before he left for work so he wouldn't have the opportunity to visit his girlfriend. She would wake my little sister and me after midnight, driving us around town in search of his truck at various women's residences when he failed to return from his shift.

Her obsession with him is beyond rational, to the point of being utterly disturbing, especially considering that the man is a known pedophile.

During the summer of my seventh-grade year, just before I turned twelve that September, I realized that my days of innocence and carefree living were behind me. I was about to start watching my little sister during the day while my father slept and my mother worked. This change came because my older sister was getting married and moving to Spain. She seemed eager to leave as quickly as possible.

My older sister had met an Air Force police officer, which was fairly easy given that we lived in a city with an Air Force base as one of its major employers. He was being deployed to Spain and had proposed to her, wanting her to accompany him. He couldn't have been older than twenty himself. She was determined to marry him and move to Spain, seeking an escape from our home and, I'm certain, from our father as well. I harbor no doubts about this.

The Christmas before this proposal, my father gave my older sister a large stuffed panda bear and neglected to buy gifts for anyone else, not even my mother or his own wife. This further solidified my doubts that there was something going on between my father and my sister.

It was later discovered that my father would buy lingerie and have my older sister model it for him. Now, you can see through lingerie, and you know what happens when men see women (in this instance, a young girl) in lingerie.

When my sister left for Spain, I was eleven, and my little sister was nine. During the summers, we spent the entire day in the pool, which was unsafe. Anything could have happened to us. The only adult at home was sleeping, and by the time one of us got into the house and got him up and out of the house into the backyard, the other one would have drowned.

I did not know how to swim well enough to save her life if something had gone wrong, especially when I was called in to handle the situation with my father. If I were not out there or I was gone too long, and she was alone for quite some time, she could drown. Sometimes, I was gone too long, and she would come searching for me. But he did not care; he was only concerned with himself and what was transpiring in that bathroom behind that closed door.

This had become the new routine. We would get up around 9:00 a.m., eat breakfast, hit the pool around 10:00 a.m., swim until I would fix us lunch around 1:00 p.m., bring it to the pool, my little sister and I would eat, and we would wait thirty minutes and get back in the pool.

It had been that way for two summers, with my older sister there to supervise. This year, it was just me and my little sister. This had been happening for about three weeks, and things were working out. My mother was concerned that I wouldn't be able to care for both of us, but I was doing a good job so far, so there was little basis for her worry. The house was clean because we spent all day in the pool, took our bathing suits off in the garage, wrapped a towel around us, and went through the back door, through the kitchen, and into the bedroom to put on clothes.

Hearing my name called that first time was no big deal. He explained he wanted to shower and wash his back; he could not reach it and needed me to wash it for him.

Okay?

I was used to seeing him nude; he was my father, and it did not seem strange to wash his back. He could not reach it, but that made sense to me. So I did what he asked of me; to my little brain, there was nothing strange with his request.

Yes, I washed his back, but there was more to it than that. Things became more sexual. He instructed me on what he wanted done and how he wanted it done and began to show me exactly what he was talking about. He then began to take pleasure in the activity. When he completed the process, he would turn himself and pull me into the shower to wash off the evidence.

Dreading the sound of the patio door sliding open, hearing my name called, and looking up and seeing him standing there, a large rock would hit the bottom of my stomach. I'd get all sweaty and anxious. As usual, I would look at my little sister and tell her to stay in the shallow end of the swimming pool and not go under the water until I got back. If she felt tired, to get out of the pool and lay down on the towel on the cement, that I would be back in a minute. It was always longer than a minute, and I sometimes heard her hollering for me at the patio door. Just a few seconds longer; do not come in the house – stay outside – you are not supposed to know.

I was required to cook his dinner for him and serve him like the dutiful little wife I was expected to play. I packed his lunch for him and saw him off to work. I managed these chores so he would not have time to see his girlfriend before work. My mother was trying to manipulate and control the whole situation through me when she was not home, but what she did not know was he was satisfying his needs in other ways with a substitute, namely me.

When the abuse began, I grew closer to my faith.

I began to feel a calling to sisterhood, to the convent. I'm not certain whether it was a true calling or if I was seeking refuge in the Divine from the unfolding events at home. My faith was all I had. In my youthful mind, I believed that by promising to take vows of celibacy and "marrying" Christ, as nuns do when they join the convent, I would be saved and spared from what was occurring at home. One Saturday evening, we attended Mass to avoid waking early on Sunday. We were preparing for the sacrament of Communion when two individuals from the congregation stood and approached the altar. They received two necklaces with large crosses from the priest, placed them around their necks, took the Body and Blood of Christ, and positioned themselves at the front of the church, ready to distribute communion. I was both shocked and appalled.

The idea of allowing commoners to handle and distribute such a sacred thing was unthinkable to me. They were not priests and did not represent Christ on earth. It took all my restraint not to cause a disturbance in the church. I walked out of the Mass immediately.

My mother was unaware of my departure. Mass was nearly over, and she didn't follow me. I faced severe reprimand when she exited the church. I explained my actions and declared I would never return, and I never did.

That day, I let my connection to the Divine wane—I disconnected to some extent. I was disillusioned with the church and with Catholicism.

For some reason, my mother didn't compel me to attend anymore, nor did she force herself to go. This might have been due to the issues we had with the teachers and her reputation as a troublemaker, or perhaps it was because her marriage was disintegrating. The last straw was when my father came into my bed one morning - naked. Upon receiving a call, he chose to answer it outside via the kitchen phone in the hallway rather than using the phone next to his bed. He walked straight into my room, went to the twin bed where I was sleeping, and lifted the sheet. He then proceeded to lie right next to me; he did not pull the sheet to cover either of us; both of us were naked, me with only my panties on and my chest bare. I could hear my heart thumping in my ears from how hard it was beating in my chest.

I did not understand what he was doing in my bed. Had he lost his mind? What was going through his head? Why was he in my bed, and what was he planning to do? Then, I heard a voice warn me, "You're in danger."

As I lay there, fear escalated with each passing moment. My palms grew sweaty, and an ominous feeling told me something terrible would happen if I didn't escape. Although he hadn't touched me yet, the weight of his gaze and his dark intentions were palpable. I was torn between running and staying. Could I move quickly enough to evade his grasp if I attempted to flee? I was paralyzed by indecision.

The conviction that remaining would lead to something horrific propelled me. The voice urged me again, "Run! Run! Run! NOW!! GO NOW!!!" In a rush, I leaped out of bed, snatched my clothes, and hastily dressed in my sister's room, all the while monitoring the hallway to ensure he wasn't following. After waking my little sister, I dressed her amidst a state of panic, continuously scanning the corridor. We left the house immediately. I instructed her never to be alone with our father and to insist on my presence if my mother ever sent them off together. I revealed to her what had just occurred but implored her to keep it from our mother to avoid repercussions. She promised secrecy.

My actions were driven by a desire to safeguard her, our mother, and myself. We sought refuge at a neighbor's house, though the remainder of that day escaped me. I vaguely recall possibly visiting the zoo with Cindy, the neighbor's daughter, and her mother, but my memory fails me—the rest of the day is a blank. My recollections are jumbled, a consequence of the trauma and dissociation I've employed over the years for self-protection.

Despite my plea, my little sister eventually told our mother.

When my mother discovered the truth about my father's actions, she must have confronted him. Whether he denied everything or remained silent, her response was drastic. In the dead of night, she pulled me from my bed, dragging me down the hallway and into the kitchen.

There, she positioned me in front of him, forcing me to act as his accuser. She prodded me to recount his actions and what he forced me to do, demanding specifics, aiming to compel his confession. Her voice rose in fury, threatening me not to lie or face her wrath.

Tears streaming, I pleaded with him to confess, to tell the truth, while he sat there, head buried in his hands, rubbing his bald head, eyes glued to the floor, unable to meet our gaze, silent amidst the chaos.

The noise seemed to amplify, my heart pounding so loudly I could hear it resounding in my ears and headbang, bang, bang, growing increasingly intense.

Frozen in place, I contemplated my chances of escape. Would the first blow come from them? Where was the nearest exit? I silently begged for honesty, for the turmoil to end.

Then, suddenly, everything quieted for a moment that seemed to stretch for minutes. In that stillness, with my father before me, his head in his hands and elbows on his knees, and my mother, clad in her blue robe with her hair in a bonnet, standing behind me, I saw white, shiny crystals floating in the air like droplets splashing from my body. My intuition whispered that this was the moment my Soul fractured, the crystals representing pieces of my Soul scattering. This image remains etched in my memory of that night.

He then rose, crossed the kitchen, and struck my mother.

She fell against the wall and slid down it. He turned away from her and took two steps. The next thing I knew, she had latched onto his back. He managed to pull her off, but she grabbed him by the testicles, trying to prevent his departure. She clamped down with a vice-like grip. Silent throughout, he uttered no confession nor denial. As he inched toward the door, dragging her along, still attached to him, she made sure to inflict pain on his most vulnerable spot, mirroring the hurt he had caused her.

As he finally reached the door, she launched herself onto his back once more. He shoved her off, and in the process, she tore the shirt from his back. She kept that shirt in her car for years, using it as a rag. I don't recall anything else from that night, but I'm certain it was tumultuous. I suspect I was interrogated for hours after revealing what had transpired between him and me. There's no doubt in my mind about that.

The moment my mother thrust me into the role of an adult, compelling him to confess his actions, she inflicted profound trauma on me. This incident not only fractured my Soul but also precipitated a bipolar episode, to which we are genetically predisposed, and established a trauma bond that linked us to her distress. She transferred her fury towards my father, her anger and disappointment in me, her shame, guilt, depression, self-loathing, and all the negative emotions generated by that moment onto me, tethering me to her anguish.

For forty-six years, I bore those burdens. I grappled with depression, anxiety, co-dependency issues, and negative energy in both my personal being and my life.

It wasn't until I finally released these burdens, sending the negative energy and the trauma that rightfully belonged to her, not me, back to her, that I was able to sever that trauma bond.

This bond and the associated negative feelings, thoughts, and energy pervaded every aspect of my life, influencing every relationship I had, whether it was love, career, or financial, impacting everything.

After that night, most of my memories became scattered and blurred, like old black and white films in a projector, with the film tearing and sliding off the reel. I've tried to locate the missing pieces, hoping to somehow tape them back together into something coherent.

Yet, the gaps are numerous, and the spaces between them are vast, making it impossible to comprehend the disjointed snippets fully. Bits and pieces are jumbled together, with shadows flitting through my mind and fleeting glimpses of what my mind's eye can recall. I've progressed so far that I'm not sure those memories are necessary anymore. Reflecting on the past, I am grateful for my ability to dissociate in order to preserve myself. My mind has likely shielded me from experiences that could have shattered me at the time. Now, fortified by strength, I can navigate through those emotions and memories as they resurface.

I am prepared to confront my Shadow Self and the traumas that have imparted valuable lessons, which have fostered healing of my Inner Child and fostered a connection with my Higher Self.

This connection brings me closer to the Divine, contributing to the healing of the collective. We are all interconnected, and through our individual healing, we contribute to the salvation of our world.

Chapter 4: Seeking Refuge, Finding Strength

I'm not certain what led my mother to seek counseling or therapy for me. I only recall visiting one therapist, a man named Dr. Duff, a few times before she abruptly stopped taking me. I liked him and felt at ease discussing the events between my father and me and my relationship with my mother.

However, there was one issue: he was relaying our conversations to my mother. I suspect that's the reason she discontinued the therapy sessions. She likely couldn't bear hearing the details. Following this, her treatment of me worsened significantly.

Reflecting on that period, I realize it marked the beginning of my first Dark Night of the Soul. I had felt the call from my Higher Self to connect with the Divine multiple times, and it was at this juncture that I reached the age needed to embark on my Spiritual Awakening Journey.

My trauma initiated my Dark Night of the Soul, signaling a call to awakening, but the damage and my disillusionment with the church obscured this path. Being so young and without protection or guidance, I was unable to see the way forward.

Starting therapy and then abruptly stopping, I believe, can be more harmful than not undergoing therapy at all. It brings deep-seated issues to the forefront, and ceasing therapy pushes them down even further, complicating future attempts to address them.

That was the problem's crux—I never processed those issues afterward. It took more than forty-six years to confront them, catalyzed by my daughter's psychology studies in college, which finally motivated me to take those steps.

My mother did file a police report but didn't pursue charges. I assume that in the mid-seventies, it was the parents' responsibility to press charges since I was too young to do so myself, and it seems the state didn't take action independently. I believe she hoped that he would return to her by not pressing charges—an utterly misguided notion. It feels as though she was willing to sacrifice me for a chance to reconcile and save her marriage with a pedophile.

Even after he stood up in a court of law, declaring he had never been married nor had five children, my mother still did not press charges and still yearned for his return. My mother, the dingbat! She wouldn't seek revenge for the sake of her daughter, but she did for her own reasons.

She reported him to the FBI for taking items from the military base where he worked. Consequently, our house was raided, his collection of tools, screws, nuts, bolts, wire, copper—everything in the garage—was confiscated, and he was arrested. My memory of that day is blurry, but I can vaguely picture looking up the driveway as men sifted through the garage, seemingly taking inventory. They were the quintessential FBI agents of that era, clad in black suits, trench coats, and those old-fashioned fedoras.

I remember how she infuriated him during their separation by selling his prized '57 Chevy for $500, including the trailer, before the property was divided. In retaliation, he dismantled the

Harley he owned, breaking it down into small pieces, and secreted it away at a girlfriend's house in boxes to prevent my mother from selling it.

My mother attempted to keep the house but couldn't afford it, and we had to leave it behind. She was particularly bitter about our new living situation (in what she referred to as "the black side of town") because I didn't want to change school districts. Additionally, my actions inadvertently deprived her of child support, which only intensified her resentment towards me.

My freshman year of school was quite eventful. One memory that stands out involves a boy I was dating and a girl from our new neighborhood whom I had befriended. I later discovered she had previously dated this boy. She was invited to his birthday party, whereas I was not.

A photo from the event captured a moment of them playfully fighting over something. She was laughing, mouth wide open, while he was behind her, arms nearly encircling her, his hands perilously close to her partially exposed boobs that were practically hanging out. Of course, I didn't like such a thing, especially when I was interested in him and everything was steady.

She and I exchanged harsh words at school over the incident. I even threatened her with a beating despite being quite timid and easily frightened myself. Somehow, she managed to align herself with the girls who bullied me, and they convinced a Mormon girl—blonde, sweet, and seemingly innocent—to intervene. She declared I'd have to confront her before reaching my initial target. I boldly accepted, though I was clearly out of my depth. The news spread like wildfire across the school within half an hour. There was no turning back now. The Mormon girl, who typically wore dresses to school, seemed like she might back out due to her attire. However, unbeknownst to me, the bullies had provided her with overalls for the fight. We met in a field behind Target after school.

I'm not one for violence and usually come out on the losing end of any physical altercation, even with my siblings, sometimes my younger sister. It required a significant amount of anger for me to engage in a fight. I insisted she strikes me first. She obliged, landing a punch on my right jaw. That was all it took to ignite my fury. I charged at her like a linebacker, bringing her down and unleashing years of pent-up anger as I pummeled her on the ground.

She cried out, claiming her shoulder was injured. The fight ended when someone pulled me off, warning me that the police or someone else was approaching. As she kicked me in the stomach and rose from the ground, a male friend came to my aid, carrying me on his back home. Living just a few blocks from Target, the journey was brief. Remarkably, no one dared to bother me for the rest of that year.

My mother and I were summoned to the principal's office the next day. Upon entering, we found the girl with both her parents, her right arm in a sling, sporting two black eyes and a swollen jaw. I, too, had a black eye and possibly a swollen cheek. I recounted the event, and my mother argued that the girl should not have intervened uninvited. She had struck me first, prompting my defense. I made sure of that and highlighted it in my argument, further bolstering my innocence.

I do not recall seeing her for the rest of the year. I do not know if it was because she changed schools or she was afraid of me. However, her parents showed up with her at my house, demanding my parents pay for her medical bills. My mother, in no uncertain terms, told them to get lost.

She asserted that she caused her own injuries by sticking her nose where it didn't belong, volunteered for a fight she couldn't handle, and needed to learn from it. Furthermore, she made it clear that if we were expected to cover her medical expenses, they would be responsible for mine.

We stood firm and did not pay her bills.

***

After my parents divorced the summer before my sophomore year, we moved into a predominantly black neighborhood following the sale of our family home. The house was on Campbell Drive. I was fourteen, nearing fifteen. We chose this neighborhood so I could remain in the same school district and graduate with my classmates from junior high. In hindsight, it seemed pointless since I had no friends to graduate with. Yet, at the time, staying in the familiar environment felt comforting, so I clung to it. Little did I know how large the high school was and that I wouldn't share any classes with those classmates, making me even lonelier without any familiar faces to mitigate my anxiety?

Perhaps moving to a different district might have altered my trajectory. However, the root of my struggles wasn't geographical but stemmed from emotional neglect, a trauma bond, and a lack of trauma therapy, all of which fueled years of depression, anxiety, and distress. I was forced to suppress the painful feelings of unworthiness without any acknowledgment of my feelings of violation and repulsion or intense self-loathing. Looking back, the emotional neglect was staggering.

Subconsciously, I was in search of emotional support, or "love," that my Inner Child desperately needed to heal from the trauma. I sought the kind of "love" my father had shown me, which was his way of expressing approval, acceptance, and validation—this was how I learned to measure my worth. My mother's behavior reinforced this, as she aimed to please my father at all costs. This dynamic deeply ingrained in me a sense of low self-esteem, self-confidence, and self-worth, rooted in the physical punishments and the derogatory statements I endured from a young age. My mother would clench her teeth when hitting me as if channeling all her energy to inflict maximum pain. The verbal abuse ranged from being told I wasn't worth the dynamite to blow me to hell to being called a brat, crybaby, bitch, and snake.

The emotional neglect soon escalated following an incident, exacerbating the situation. After the problems with my father, the names changed to "whore" and "slut." All the while, my Higher Self was beckoning me towards the Divine. As a child, I felt called to follow Christ without fully understanding the journey ahead. Now, ripe for that journey but deeply traumatized and broken, I was unaware of the challenging path I was choosing.

My older sister was an avid pot smoker, and she introduced me to smoking grass at the age of fifteen. Initially, I didn't really enjoy it. It took a few sessions before I started to feel any effects, but it definitely stimulated my appetite—a dead giveaway. She always cautioned me, "Don't go straight for the kitchen." She believed our mother was aware of what was happening, but I don't think she had a clue until I was well into my early twenties. That's when she began to allow us to smoke grass in front of her while playing Up Words, a Scrabble-like game that involves building words upwards as well as across and down. It was a cool game, and we all enjoyed playing it together.

Occasionally, my mother would take a "hit." It was hilarious watching her attempt to smoke in the same manner she did cigarettes, puffing and immediately blowing out the smoke. She was never much of a smoker or drinker; she couldn't handle alcohol, much less anything else.

The day the divorce was either granted or finalized, I came home from school to find my mother in her bedroom. She was lying face down at the foot of her bed, her head hanging over the edge with a wet rag in her hand, moaning. My older sister was there, gently rubbing her back, and the room was filled with the smell of rank alcohol.

My sister looked up at me, told me to "get the hell out," grabbed the door from my hand, slammed it shut, and locked it. My mother had consumed so much Vodka and Seven (Vodka, 7 UP with red grenadine) that she must have been close to alcohol poisoning. She was vomiting and dry-heaving. My sister blamed me for our mother's condition, asserting that if I had never spoken up, she wouldn't have gotten divorced. I'm not sure how my mother got home—whether someone she was celebrating or mourning brought her home, called a cab, or my sister brought her.

Starting my sophomore year in high school, my focus was solely on getting my driver's license, obtaining a car, graduating, and escaping my mother's home and her control. At that moment, my entire life revolved around surviving these grueling teenage years and planning my getaway. I aimed to avoid bullies whenever possible and hoped not to make any enemies, which was easier in this larger school that combined students from several junior high schools. Perhaps I even entertained the hope of making a few friends that year.

I remember the first day - it was so overwhelming!!

The butterflies in my chest - I did not know at the time that what I was experiencing was a panic attack. I just knew then it was fluttering so fast I almost could not catch my breath!

I was full of fear and anxiety - would I find my locker? Would I find my classes and make it there before the bell? Which hallway was I in? What staircase is this? Am I on the right side of the building?

Apart from all this running through my head, I was also constantly on the lookout for bullies while trying to avoid running into people.

Wow!

It kind of gives me anxiety just thinking about it!

I had started babysitting for this police officer who lived down the street from our house. It was usually on Friday and Saturday nights only because he worked the three to eleven shift, and his wife either worked or would go out on those nights.

Needless to say, it took me a lot to convince my mother to let me do it. It helped that the job was for a police officer and was only two houses down, which made her relent.

I met a boy not too long after we moved into the new home. He did not live in our neighborhood, and I cannot remember how we met, but he was the boy who would take my virginity.

He was not particularly handsome, and I wasn't all that taken by him. He was not the love of my life either; he was someone else whom I had met a year earlier at our old house. This boyfriend really was not anyone that special, and we had only seen each other for a month or so. I was fifteen, and he was sixteen. He had come to my babysitting job, and we did the deed after the kids had been put to bed.

When it happened, I remember thinking, *"Is that all there is? That's what all the commotion is about? I do not feel any different. Shouldn't I feel like a different person? Did I do something wrong? Did he do something wrong? Why does it not feel special like everyone said it is supposed to feel? What a letdown."*

I was so naive that I did not know women were supposed to have orgasms. Hell, I did not even know what an orgasm was. I probably thought that was only for men if I knew what it was. All I was worried about at the time was not getting pregnant. That was my only concern.

Everything would have been solid and under the radar if my older sister hadn't shown up out of the blue (she always had a way of showing up when I didn't want her around) and if he hadn't left the condom in the ashtray like some idiot we would have gotten away with it! It seems that since the beginning, I picked nothing but losers. I do not blame the decision to have sex so early in age on anyone but myself. It was my decision. However, I do believe that had I not been exposed to certain acts of a sexual nature at such an early age, I would not have chosen to lose my virginity, and I would not have gotten pregnant at such a young age.

My sister showed up in a wake-up call – unheeded. Higher Self was telling me I was headed for trouble – to slow down and look at what I was doing and where I was going. I was so blinded by youth and inexperience. I was searching but in the wrong direction. I was looking for comfort, love, refuge, and protection.

My sister was dating the brother of one of my ex-husbands (we will call him "my crush" to keep it uncomplicated) (we have two nieces in common - as they were once common law married - long story). When I met this ex-husband, we were around fourteen, and I fell for him the moment I saw him (he looked like a teenage Michael Landon – hair and all). Still, my sister and his brother knew how we felt.

They kept us from each other in order to avoid any further complications from my mother, as she hated his older brother. They wanted to avoid the additional trouble there would have been if we had begun dating. That didn't mean the two of us didn't do our damnedest to try and see each other when we could and try to find a way to date and be together.

I was babysitting one night, and my crush showed up out of nowhere with beer and a little grass. I was surprised and overjoyed when I opened that door!

We started drinking, and things got out of hand. Mind you, I had never drunk before. To this day, I do not remember anything past the first sip of the first beer. I was told I drank a six-pack by myself; I was dancing on the coffee table and proclaiming my undying love for my crush to his face. I guess I was a bit too much, and he couldn't handle the situation. Because he was at a cop's house, he called his brother and my sister.

Soon after that incident, his older brother and my older sister arrived at the house. I vaguely remember someone holding my hair back as I vomited and being made to drink a concoction of milk mixed with hot sauce, raw egg, and sugar, which only worsened my condition. The room was spinning, and I found myself lying on the bathroom floor, unwilling to move due to the severe nausea and stomach pain from retching.

The next thing I knew, the police officer was waking me up. I was on the living room floor with a large green Tupperware bowl under my face. I felt utterly demolished as if a Mack truck had run over me. My mouth tasted horrendous, and my head throbbed with pain. When he inquired about what had happened, I managed to say I was sick and felt terrible. I wasn't sure whether the bathroom had been cleaned of vomit or if they had left it as it was. All I knew was that I felt miserable and yearned to go home to bed.

I don't remember walking back to my house, three doors up, or getting into bed. The dry heaves persisted for a couple of days, a sign of alcohol poisoning, though I was unaware of it at the time. I never babysat for him again, and oddly, I don't recall facing any consequences, so I'm unsure if the officer ever pieced it together or chose not to tell my mother. Since then, I haven't touched alcohol and have lived soberly. I now understand that the Islamic religion prohibits alcohol because it's believed to allow demons to take control of the Soul, hence the term "spirits." My Higher Self was protecting me from malevolent spirits, demons, and entities from other planes and dimensions due to my gifts. That's why that was my sole experience with alcohol, as well as my attempts with non-prescription drugs. I couldn't take them; they made me sick, so I never tried them again.

A couple of weeks later, my crush came over around noon one day with his brother and my older sister and asked me to go to the drive-in with them that evening. I was so excited to go.

Mind you, I had no memory of what had transpired the night I had gotten plastered. I did not remember anything except the small snippets of getting sick and the major hangover I had the days following the incident. Thinking back now, my crush probably wanted to spend some sober time with me to tell me he felt the same way that I had proclaimed to him.

However, my boyfriend at the time came to the house unexpectedly, uninvited and unwelcomed. My sister did not want my crush and me to be alone, so she told my boyfriend about the movie, and he wanted to go. I couldn't find an excuse not to take him with us, so he tagged along, as did my little sister (my older sister was always trying to hook up my crush with my little sister??).

I couldn't find any excuse to find time to be alone with my crush, and I spent the whole night feeling miserable. My crush and I didn't cross each other's paths very often, mainly because his family was troubled, and my mother couldn't stand them. We wouldn't really speak our truth to each other until much later in life.

One night after this incident, and maybe because of it, my boyfriend came to visit, and we had a disagreement. During this argument, my older sister—she always had some reason to pull my love interests aside and try to seduce them—took him outside to the backyard. Supposedly, they sat on a blanket, smoked a joint, and talked (for 3 hours—his entire visit). I went to bed in protest.

She knew my insecurities and what had happened between my father and me, and it was like she was using that to torture me. As though she was—like my mother—jealous of the abuse that occurred with my father—like she had wished it had been her or that it should have been her in my shoes or how dare I take her place!!!

Fucking weird now that I think about it!! It was as though— you took my man, so I am going to take yours!!

Sick—just sick!!!My sister tried to set my crush up with my little sister on a couple of occasions. He was wrong for me, but he was okay with her. One time, on a camping trip when I had already been asked to go, I had cleared it with my mother and was the one who was supposed to go. My older sister purposely left 3 hours early before I made it home from work to make sure I did not get to go, and she took my little sister with her. Both my crush and I were tricked and pissed off. She has always been a real bitch to me. Always working against me in one way or another. I can remember how much pleasure she would take beating me up when we were small children. She would grit her teeth when she hit me like she wanted to hit me as hard as she could, just like my mother did when she hit me.

She was a stripper back then (which I believe stemmed from her encounters with our father), so she thought she was just God's gift to men. She could con men out of their money for watered-down drinks, so she thought she could con my love interests into cheating on me. I couldn't prove it, and he always denied it (she denied it too - but the Divine has told me my intuition has been right on the money all these years), but I have always thought "something" happened. I'm not saying sex, but something happened.

I was no longer attracted to my boyfriend because of the little bit of interest my crush had shown in me and my suspicions of what had occurred between him and my sister. I was going to break it off with him and really go after my crush, whether my sister or his brother liked it or not.

Then, my boyfriend had an accident in his father's garage right before I could break up with him. He was working on a car, and the light had blown out of the gas heater. He went to light it, and it blew up and caught him on fire. He was badly burned. I stayed with him because he was afraid I would break up with him due to the injuries to his face. I doctored his injuries and took care of him while he healed. It took several months. I still cared for him, stayed with him, and nursed him through it. Things just were not the same between us after the incident with my sister and his accident, as well as the fact that I had been interested in my crush for over a year. I just couldn't break up with him during his recovery. I waited a couple of weeks, and then I broke up with him. When we were older, I ran into him. He had gained a lot of weight, and I almost did not recognize him. I later discovered he had become an alcoholic and had moved to some small town down south, gotten married, and had a couple of children.

Soon after breaking up with my boyfriend, I landed a job setting up the C R Anthony's store from scratch in our city, later transitioning to a salesperson role. This clothing store emerged before the mall era, filled with nothing but clothes and shoe racks that needed tagging, marking, and shelving. Earning $2.10 an hour, I felt quite accomplished.

Technically, workers under sixteen needed a work permit, but I flew under the radar, working without one. With just a few months before my sixteenth birthday, I fudged the application details, and my secret remained undiscovered.

Entering my junior year, I had just turned sixteen and was working legally. My sights were set on obtaining a driver's license and enrolling in a driver's education class as one of my electives, along with French.

My mother's attempt to immerse us in the Mormon church had failed spectacularly. Drawn to the French language, I was intrigued by my teacher's plans for a field trip to France. Despite my longing to join, the dual barriers of my mother's permission and the financial cost made it an unreachable dream.

Yet, this period marked a peak in my life in terms of productivity, independence, and overcoming adversity. For once, I felt a sense of self-confidence and self-worth. Having prayed for my job in the preceding months, I achieved it, though my prayers for anything else were sparse, and my connection with Christ and the Divine was nearly non-existent. I treated the Divine as a celestial Santa Claus—adhering to the "ask and ye shall receive" mantra.

While working, I encountered a boy who had been a senior during my sophomore year. He was a former baseball team member and had graduated the year before. He entered the store with his best friend, who was dating a girl from one of my classes, a couple I had noticed before his graduation.

They had been together since junior high, and she was anticipating an engagement ring. She became my link to meeting my next romantic interest. We were formally introduced a few weeks later.

Chapter 5: Unraveling Bonds

"You, God, are my God, earnestly I seek you; I thirst for you, my whole being longs for you, in a dry and parched land where there is no water."

—Psalm 63 Verse 1

Change in life is always sudden and comes without any warning. It is weird how, in one moment, everything is working out, and the very next, the same things seem to pull you into a sinkhole, dragging you under where no light can reach you.

This unpredictability scares me. It terrifies me how the things that meant the world to me suddenly become the cause of my suffering.

I started dating the baseball star in August 1978 and got pregnant in December of the same year. We hadn't been dating long before we began having sex, and I was aware of the risk of getting pregnant.

My previous boyfriend had always been responsible for protection during our intimate moments. Thus, I believed that protection was a responsibility he should have assumed, especially since he was eighteen, and my mother was not going to discuss birth control with me, let alone provide it.

She didn't know I wasn't a virgin, and I had no intention of telling her. He had been in a rather serious relationship for two years during high school before dating me. I guess she was either using birth control, or they were simply fortunate. I was still quite naive regarding sexual matters. He was only the second person I had ever been intimate with, and I hadn't been with anyone but my first partner three months prior to being with him. My mother once caught us in a heavy petting session in the living room, leading to me being grounded and prohibited from seeing him for several weeks. She had her suspicions about us being sexually active. She was particularly worried about "car dates," convinced they would inevitably lead to pregnancy. During our enforced separation, I'm sure I drove his family to distraction with my constant phone calls, eager to speak to him. Being a young, insecure, and overly dramatic teenage girl with a deep crush on their beloved son and forced to be apart from "the man I loved," I likely called several times a day. Remember, this was a time before cell phones.

Before I had my children, my menstrual cycles were like clockwork. I missed my period by two weeks, and I'm certain my mother noticed. My older sister suddenly showed a keen interest in my well-being, undoubtedly prompted by my mother. That day, I confided in her that I was late. She purchased a home pregnancy test for me, which turned out positive.

She persuaded me to inform our mother, hoping she would have time to temper her anger before returning home from work. When I called to break the news, her reaction was far from calm. I could feel her fury through the phone, her voice laden with anger; I wouldn't have been surprised if everyone in her large office building had heard her yelling and cursing at me.

I feared I wouldn't survive her wrath.

At the latest, I had told my mother about my predicament around three hours ago. When she got home, she was still furious!

I didn't know whether to run, hide, or just cower in the corner with my back to her and prepare to be hit when she came through the door. I received a yardstick beating. She smacked me so hard with it that she broke it over my knees while I was seated in a chair. She had to penalize me for defrauding her of two years of child support in addition to my pregnancy at sixteen.

I was nothing more to her than a monthly check. She was having trouble when her alimony ended six months earlier. She was going to give me or the baby the whore treatment—or both!

Her answer was to have me marry him and threaten to report the boy for statutory rape. My mother was bound and determined that he was going to create an honest lady out of her "little girl" and give her grandbaby a respectable last name, or he was going to jail. His parents disapproved of the idea of getting married, but they didn't want their son to end up in jail.

If, at that age, the idea of being in love, getting married, and starting a family was all fantasy, I did not want him to end up in jail even if I felt I was in love with him. I was also unsure about being compelled to marry. However, it wasn't exactly a fantastic way to begin a marriage, was it? Fearing incarceration?

Me? I was in a magical place from my youth!

My mother is an absolute winner—she can intimidate someone into marriage and impose her views on me and everyone else! Given that we were forced into marriage (among other issues, of course), it is understandable why the union did not succeed! I had already reached the end of my teenage years! This Dark Night of the Soul was growing darker and darker. I'm sure I was praying, but I think I was praying for marriage and a child—for guidance on whether to marry, have a child, or take some other action. I also recall that I was fearful. I had no idea what lay ahead for me.

Looking back over the years, the marriage was a joke, a complete sham. It served only to give my daughter her legal last name. From the beginning, I was seen as a joke by her father and his family—the girl from the wrong side of the tracks, deemed ignorant, with no proper upbringing. I was merely someone to sleep with until he found something better or until he grew tired of me. He made a mistake by not using condoms; I got pregnant, and he ended up with a baby and a wife he didn't want. OOPS!!!

His parents even tried to claim she wasn't his child, framing our union as a marriage of convenience to keep their son out of jail. At my wedding, my mother ensured my younger sister outshone me. In a bid to punish and belittle me, she refused to buy me a wedding dress. Instead, she bought my little sister an elaborate Southern Belle bridesmaid dress with a hoop skirt, ensuring she was the center of attention on what should have been my day. I was left to wear my freshman prom dress, which, thankfully, was white and still fit.

My mother didn't allow me a moment to shine on my day. She complained and made a scene throughout, embarrassing me for the entire four hours she deemed "wasted and could have been better spent." The ceremony itself was modest, and my mother ensured it was as inexpensive as possible. We were married by a part-time preacher in the makeshift chapel of his garage. Present were me and my daughter's father, his parents, my mother, my little sister, possibly my older sisters, my sister-in-law, and a few of my nieces and nephews.

My brother may have given me away, but I can't say for sure. No effort was made to make the occasion even slightly celebratory. I never had a birthday party, except for my 45th, which featured a cheap homemade cake and family attendance. In contrast, my little sister celebrated her birthday every year.

No wedding photos were taken, and it reminded me of a shotgun wedding. It would have been better to go before the Justice of the Peace at the Courthouse and then have lunch at Denny's. It didn't mean anything as usual because it involved me—just a bland, thrown-together ceremony.

The reception was at my mother's run-down, dirty house. His parents considered it on the wrong side of the tracks, essentially the ghetto. There was no food, just a makeshift bar—there might have been a cake. My oldest sister's boyfriend, who was a part-time bartender, served drinks. My husband's parents, who were very racist, did not stay long. My new husband may have left with them because my oldest sister's boyfriend at the time was African American. I can't even remember if we spent our wedding night together. I think we lived apart until we found somewhere to live together.

My oldest sister had been living in a one-bedroom duplex. When she moved out, somehow, we moved into it. It was extremely small but affordable, and I turned it into a nice little home. If I remember correctly, he worked in the oil field and was gone during the week and home on weekends. We spent Sundays with his parents every single Sunday. This was why he sent me packing with my daughter six months after she was born.

During my pregnancy, I had pre-eclampsia, a condition involving water retention and high blood pressure that causes stress on the baby. I was bedridden for several weeks at the end of my pregnancy under doctor's orders. My mother would occasionally stop by on her way to work and bring me things I craved, like blueberries, cantaloupe, and watermelon. Probably not the best for someone retaining water like a sponge.

She seemed excited about the baby's birth, though I don't know why, especially considering her reaction to the pregnancy and her feelings toward me. She spent nine months hitting garage sales to buy clothes, blankets, and such to prepare for the baby's arrival. Back then, they couldn't tell you the baby's gender before birth, so she bought gender-neutral items until my daughter arrived in September 1979.

That was the closest I had ever felt to my mother. But once my daughter was born, everything changed. She reverted to the cruel, cold person she had been my entire life. Once she got her hands on my daughter, she took control of everything: her feeding, bathing, dressing—everything. Then she complained about it and accused me of being an absent, unfit mother. She was a controlling, manipulative, lying narcissist. I didn't realize that until about a decade ago when my daughter explained those traits.

For example, after a traumatic experience during the birth of my daughter, I was just seventeen years old myself, needing comfort and reassurance. I endured thirty-six hours of labor, with medical staff inducing and then stopping my labor repeatedly.

The stress of childbirth was intense: a c-section surgery while being wide awake. I was terrified because I had never undergone surgery before, and they were going to cut my body open while I was wide awake!

The whole time I was in the operating room, the boards they had strapped my arms to kept clanging on the metal tables underneath because my arms were jumping up and down from the shaking—I was so nervous.

After the surgery, I looked at my mother and asked her, "Isn't she beautiful?" At the time, my mother said, "Yes, yes, she is!" But she later admitted she just said that because she didn't want to tell me that my daughter looked like a lizard.

You see, my daughter had laid in the birth canal for 36 hours, and they had to reshape her head. It was just one more thing she said to make me feel awful about myself and my child.

She never had anything nice to say to me, about me, or for me. She never built up my confidence, self-esteem, or self-worth. Never told me she was proud of me or my accomplishments. Never validated me or anything I did. I spent my entire life trying to prove my worth to her, which was a waste of time and mental anguish. It never happened. I was never validated, acknowledged, or emotionally nurtured.

The next day after the delivery, my husband visited me when two women entered my room. One, a tall blonde, took him out into the hall, and the other, a medium-height brunette, stayed with me. My husband and the blonde were gone for about twenty minutes. The girl and I sat in silence the entire time.

I do not recall if he returned to stay, if he left right after they did, or if he stayed and visited. I did not realize it was his ex-girlfriend from high school who had left him for a wealthy Iranian man and had a baby before I did until much later. I guess she wanted him back, and that's when their affair started.

Looking back on it now, that's probably why he wanted me gone so soon after my daughter was born. He was already seeing her; they married soon after our divorce, and she was already pregnant with their son.

The first Christmas I spent with my husband and in-laws after my daughter was born revealed exactly what he and his family thought of me. I rarely had nice clothes growing up, especially ones I didn't have to share.

We always bought secondhand clothes or off the sales racks, and I never had anything. His family, being upper-middle to upper-class, had purchased some very nice clothes for me, and I was extremely excited. When I tried on the clothes and realized the pants were too long, I showed them the outfit by lifting my foot (I can't remember if I had my shoe on) and placing it on the side of the couch.

He looked at my foot, then at me, screwed up his face, and said, "Were you born in a barn?"

I was so embarrassed and hurt that I ran into one of the bedrooms and started to cry. A few minutes later, his mother came in to try to calm me down. I do not recall anything she said or leaving that room because I am sure I was embarrassed not only by what he said and how he said it but also by what I did and my reaction.

They had more moments of being mean and hateful to me than not. I do not remember much more about our time together because our marriage was short-lived, and we only lived together for a little over a year. We spent every Sunday with his parents; it was always the same thing—Sunday dinner: pot roast, potatoes, carrots, salad, and iced tea.

It was a Sunday in March 1980 when I wanted to spend a day alone with just him, me, and our daughter. He became extremely angry about it; I couldn't figure out why. He wouldn't or couldn't give me an explanation and told me to leave and take her with me; our marriage was over. He used the first excuse he could grab onto to get me out so he could move on with his concubine.

Looking back on it now, what a lame excuse! I had my mother come to get me, and I did not see him again until June of that year.

When my husband kicked me out and sent me back to my mother's with a six-month-old baby in tow—no job, no education—within a month, my mother enrolled me at the Oklahoma City Vo-Tech through the Department of Human Services Unwed Mothers program, where I received my GED and a general office clerical certificate.

Keeping her happy was not easy. Trying to live by her rules, I was still a child by age but an adult because I had a child of my own. I wanted to stand up to her and be my own person, and I tried to do that. But whenever I tried to assert myself, she would threaten to turn me in to the Department of Human Services for child neglect or child abuse, or she would threaten to take my daughter from me to force me to do what she wanted and to keep me under her control. I lived with my mother and my little sister while attending school and getting my life together until my daughter was two and a half years old. My mother, always looking to hurt me in any way she could, frequently threatened to take my daughter away from me. She never acted on these threats, nor did she ever take my daughter. Despite the challenges, I graduated at the same time as my class in May 1980. I took my daughter from my mother's home, and she never "raised" her again—a term my mother always chose to use.

She co-signed a $1,000 car loan for me so I could get back and forth to school. Managing car payments, buying baby care items like diapers, purchasing groceries, trying to help with house expenses, all on $200.00 in child support a month, and going to school at the age of seventeen was overwhelming. Trying to be an adult while still in the body and mindset of a child was incredibly difficult. She gave no leniency whatsoever. Constant criticisms—I was never good enough, I was not going to amount to anything, I was a slut, a whore, etc. She couldn't understand why I stayed out all night or didn't come home all weekend. But inevitably, she would complain about that, too!

Still underage, my mother used my naivety to keep me under her control. She made sure I was on birth control the minute my daughter was born. Even though I was married, she still made decisions for me. His parents also made decisions for us. Neither of us knew what we were doing. And she continued to make decisions for me when I was forced to move back home.

I was introduced to a young Green Beret, who had recently left the military, by my older sister and her partner at the time. He worked with this guy and thought we would hit it off. He was five years older than me. I was only seventeen then, but age did not matter back then, especially in the early '80s. While dating this guy, one night, my mother called and told me to check and lock all the windows in the house after the man I was seeing had dropped me off and left. She had seen a shadow over her shoulder for the past couple of days and wanted me to secure the house before going to bed.

My mother was psychic as well. She had a dark premonition that something was going to happen and wanted to ensure I was secure at home, especially since I would be alone until she returned from work. I checked and locked the windows in the house but unknowingly missed one in my bedroom. My mother startled me when she arrived home after her night shift around midnight. Knowing I had class early the next day, she took my daughter to bed with her so I could sleep soundly.

At around two-thirty in the morning, I was woken up by a weight on my chest. When I opened my eyes, it was completely dark, as if I were blind. I moved the upper part of my body when a hand covered my mouth, and a man's voice told me not to make a noise, or he would slit my throat from ear to ear and kill everyone in the house.

He had been inside long enough to navigate through my room full of boxes and to discover there were others in the house, namely my mother and daughter. He had also shut my bedroom door. I cooperated with him and did what I was told to save my life and my family's lives. He told me to remove my panties and tampon and proceeded to violate me. He was having difficulty, so he forced himself and tore me open. After completing his crime, he shoved me into my closet and closed the door. I waited until I thought he was gone, and as I ran from my closet to find my mother, I ran directly into my bedroom door. My mother, upon waking, insisted I was just dreaming until she saw the blood that covered me from my waist to my knees. I was on my menstrual cycle, and he had indeed torn me as well.

My oldest sister must have startled him when she returned from a night out around 3:30 a.m. My mother instructed my sister to call the police. When they arrived, they transported me to the hospital in the back of a police cruiser. I had to recount my story to ten different policemen, each one observing my vaginal examination. It felt like being violated repeatedly as all these men looked at my private parts and listened to me repeat my story as if deriving some perverse satisfaction from it.

My husband, who had left for boot camp shortly after we separated, was home at the time. Despite our separation, we were still legally married, and I found myself desperately wanting him by my side. When he and his father arrived at the emergency room, the police informed them that I had been raped by a Black man.

His father declared that I was now dirty and no longer pure, refusing to let my husband see me and promptly leaving the hospital. This event significantly contributed to what I can only describe as my darkest period, yet I continued to dissociate and ignore my inner call for healing, adding to the heavy burden I would carry for most of my life.

A few days later, my mother, perhaps feeling a semblance of empathy or compassion, shared with me her own experience of being raped while we lived in Illinois.

My father, who was supposed to pick her up from her waitressing job, was preoccupied, despite not working, and had sent a neighbor or friend instead. This individual raped her on the way home. I got the impression my father did not believe her, and I don't think she ever reported it. I don't recall much about the conversation as she shared her story.

Perhaps because she had never shown any empathy or compassion towards me before, I couldn't muster any for her, making it impossible to connect or believe that this revelation could bring us any closer, given our strained relationship.

It took me a couple of months to be able to go back to school and graduate from my clerical courses because I developed a fear of every black man I encountered, a fear that lasted for years. I finally returned to school in September, completed my clerical course, graduated, and found employment. As usual, my achievement went unrecognized. I was simply told to go out and find a job so I could start paying more rent, covering utilities, and buying food.

I lost my relationship with the Green Beret because of the rape. I couldn't bring myself to have intercourse with him or any man after that. The mere thought of sex, being touched, or removing my clothes in front of someone was unbearable. Several months passed, and I sank into a deep depression. Throughout my life, I've experienced these periods of depression, but somehow, I always managed to pull myself out, or so I thought. Looking back, I realize I wasn't truly overcoming these depressive episodes; I was dissociating, a coping mechanism that only worsened with each subsequent depression and trauma.

I didn't know I was being divorced until I received the papers from my husband, who was overseas. Heartbroken and devastated, I thought my world was ending. I believed I could never survive without him—a thought I now see as overly dramatic. Despite everything, I still harbored feelings for him, perhaps because we had a daughter together and felt an eternal bond.

My first real love? I think not. I was young and naive, soon to be nineteen, with no real understanding of life.

My mother, equally inexperienced in the real world, offered no guidance. I was on my own. Unable to afford an attorney, I was taken advantage of during the divorce proceedings, relinquishing my rights to claim my daughter on my income taxes, among other concessions. I allowed his parents' visitation out of kindness, but it was not appreciated.

He exploited me throughout her childhood. My mother never supported me in any significant life decision. I learned not to confide in her with any details of my life, as she would inevitably share and gossip about them. She couldn't be trusted with anything.

The investigation into the rape stalled for a while. I was interviewed several times, and they even attempted hypnosis, which only made me fall asleep. However, they insisted it was helpful. They showed me some mug shots, and I identified a man who looked familiar out of the three they presented.

His name was Curtis Antonio Lyons, a name I'll never forget. From what I later understood, the authorities were eager to apprehend him as he had been a suspect in numerous incidents, including entering a little girl's room through her window, just down the street from me, a few weeks prior to my assault. I attended the trial by myself, without any family support. Testifying alone in the courtroom, I was subjected to harsh scrutiny, accused of inviting a man into my room at 2:00 a.m. through my bedroom window for sex simply because I was eighteen years old with a baby and had become pregnant at 16. The fact that I had been forcibly confined in my closet and had been so violently torn that I required stitches seemed irrelevant. Throughout this ordeal, there was no one to comfort me, no one to hold my hand—I faced it all utterly alone.

Later, I heard rumors, the truth of which I cannot confirm, that my brother was present in the courtroom, watching both the assailant and me with a gun in his truck parked outside.

The defendant was not sentenced to any time; the judge dismissed the case with prejudice, meaning it could not be refiled against him. Critical evidence—hairs, semen, sheets, my panties—all mysteriously vanished.

After enduring a brutal testimony and being humiliated and persecuted for his crime, he was released, free as a bird. This experience shattered my faith in the justice system. Once again, I confronted this disappointment in solitude, with no one to share my anger and despair.

My depression worsened, yet I suppressed it, ignored it, and dissociated, further darkening my Soul. When overwhelmed, I allowed myself only brief moments of tears before forcing myself to move on. Raised by my mother to believe "there was no time for tears" and threatened to "stop crying or I'll give you something to cry about," I learned early on to stifle my emotions despite having legitimate reasons for my sorrow. This upbringing makes it difficult for me to allow myself more than a few moments of tears now, fearing that once I start, I might not be able to stop. I understand that crying is part of the healing process, yet I struggle with it. If I were to cry every time I felt moved—be it by sadness, happiness, or any other emotion—I fear I'd be in tears constantly.

As an empath, I absorb not only my own emotions but those of others as well, which can be overwhelming. Experiencing sadness, anger, and depression from both myself and those around me forces me to distance myself from others to avoid being drained by their emotions, especially as I work through my own healing process.

I decided to try and get over my assault and the negative outcome of the trial by attempting to start living my life again, to start acting like myself. I began going out again, meeting people, and trying to get back into my groove, all without therapy or any kind of counseling, which, in hindsight, I desperately needed.

Given the incidents with my father and this rape, therapy was not just a recommendation; it was a necessity. However, I was learning how to dissociate, making it increasingly easier just to ignore my issues.

One afternoon, in an attempt to reclaim some normalcy, I put on a bathing suit and pulled my car into the front yard to wash it. At that time, I was a nineteen-year-old girl trying to find peace. However, my mother's return from her errands quickly shattered that peace.

She saw me and said, "It's no wonder you got raped, being in this neighborhood and out here dressed like that." It was victim-blaming, reminiscent of the situation involving my father, and probably reflective of how my father had responded to her own rape. She constantly put me down, never offering anything positive to say to me or about me. Ridicule was all I ever received from her. Despite the lack of support, I moved forward from the assault the best I could on my own. It took a whole year to discover that it was okay for a man to touch me again and to understand that there was a significant difference between the touch of assault and the touch of intimacy.

While looking for employment, I went into a local grocery store to put in an application. As I waited to see the manager, a song played through the store's speakers, and I found myself singing along. A produce clerk walked by and heard me singing. You see, back when I was a young child, I harbored a deep-seated belief that I was meant to be someone important someday, that I was destined to be known by thousands of people.

At that time, I thought my calling was to be a singer because that was my passion. He approached me and asked if I had ever sung in a band. I hadn't. He was impressed with my voice and range and mentioned that his band was looking for a female lead vocalist for a small five-week tour that was coming up in a few weeks. He wanted to know if I would audition. Being nineteen and thrilled that someone was interested in me and my talent, I jumped at the chance.

I tried out but failed miserably. The truth is, I can't read music; I learn pitches, notes, and lyrics by sound and repetition. That's how I learned to play the clarinet—I never actually read the music. I learned the keys on the clarinet but never how to read them on the music sheet. I just couldn't seem to grasp it. I couldn't translate the notes to my fingers or my voice.

I received a call a few days later regarding the job. If I wanted it, practice was scheduled for Friday at 6:00 p.m. I was thrilled! My big chance had arrived. I couldn't wait to share the news with my mother and family. When I did, my mother's reaction shattered me.

Standing up, she sneered at me, her face contorted in the meanest expression I'd ever seen. It was as though she was questioning my worthiness.

"You? What makes you think YOU could ever be a singer?" she said. "That's just a pipe dream. You'll never amount to anything like that. You're not good enough to be a star! With a child to care for, you need to stop daydreaming, plant your feet on the ground, grow up, and get a job!"

Her words crushed my dream, leaving me feeling like I could never rise above being a mediocre 9-to-5 secretary.

This marked the beginning of a cycle. Offers came, but I had to turn them down. I'd be near success, only to stumble at the finish line. It felt like my mother's curse from birth, intensifying with each potential success. Reluctantly, I informed the band, let go of my dream, and pushed past the pain of my mother's words.

I began to rebel, meeting a guy who drove a Baja Bug. It had a brown with a gold speck paint job, and he was attractive—tall, with long curly hair and hazel eyes. I was smitten. He was perhaps the best-looking guy I'd dated, fitting my type perfectly at the time. We met when I was twenty, and he became a significant part of my life for three years, helping me raise my daughter. Yet, my family's narrative paints a different picture. According to them, they raised my daughter until she was three, implying my absence. That's not entirely accurate.

I lived with my little sister and mother until my daughter was two and a half, so I was present regularly. My mother took care of my sister's children and grandchildren, not mine.

Let's set the record straight, shall we?

He and I met at a Sonic; we were parked next to each other in the stalls. All we could see of each other were our eyes. It was November, and it was beginning to turn winter, so it was too cold to roll the windows down completely.

Our first date was extremely memorable, and it revealed his true character. After our first date, I knew he could be trusted and was a good man. He had picked me up, and we had gone out for a burger. Remember, I was only about nineteen - twenty years old. I'm not old enough to drink, so he can't take me to the bar.

We went out and shot some pool, and he had a couple of beers. He asked me if I had ever tried a quaalude, and I never had, so I was willing to give it a try, wanting to impress and all - stupid decision. He offered one - I took it. We went to one of his friend's houses. Things were good for about an hour.

I made it to their bathroom, but he had to help me out of their house and practically carry me to the car. I told him I could not go home because my mother could not see me like that. I was sick to my stomach, and I could not function. I do not remember how, when, where - nothing!!!

I woke up the next morning - almost in the afternoon - fully clothed except for my shoes, looking like a burnt souffle!! He was on the other bed, completely dressed, watching me sleep. I was so embarrassed I wanted to die!!! I could not remember what happened! All I could do was keep apologizing. Bits and pieces, nothing coherent!

I thought he would never want to see me again! I guess he found it funny, cute, or endearing because we spent three, almost four, years together. I have more fond memories than bad of our time together. When this man and I had been dating for about a year, we had an argument, and I left the house we were living in together.

I ended up at a truck stop down the highway and went in to have a cup of coffee. I met an old trucker (he was at least in his mid to late sixties) and his team driver. They were heading to California and asked me if I wanted to go.

My daughter was with my mother. I had nothing holding me here and had just left my partner's home with whom I had an uncertain future. So, with only a change of clothes, a pack of cigarettes, and no money in my pocket, I parked my car in the back of the truck stop parking lot, jumped in the semi-truck, and took off for California.

I took some big risks back then. I could have been kidnapped, sex trafficked, killed, or anything, but I really did not care. You know, I do not remember anyone getting upset or being concerned about where I had been that week. I do not recall anyone reporting me as missing or asking me where I had been, in fact. I am sure my partner at the time was concerned about where I had been, but I am pretty sure my mother had no concern whatsoever. That is the riskiest thing I have ever done in my life, and looking back on it, it's not the brightest thing either. I'm sure I was having a manic episode at the time.

I was working at Oklahoma Farm Bureau Insurance company, and we were living in a small house on a street named Rickenbacker. My daughter was attending nursery school/preschool. My boyfriend worked as a mechanic and sold drugs on the side to supplement our income.

Once reconciled, we spent most of our relationship smoking marijuana and having friends over to visit. We would sit around and talk about what we thought was important at the time. We did not talk much about politics, religion, or the current news.

We talked mostly about music, fashion, what we were feeding our kids, what we were doing the next week, the different strains of marijuana that they were bringing in over the border, and when the next shipment of cocaine was expected. It was the eighties.

You could be talking about laundry detergent, and the next sentence out of your mouth would be about taking a gram over to Billy Bob's house, and then you could go right back to talking about the next big floor cleaner you used yesterday—just normal everyday activity and conversation in those days.

My boyfriend was running drugs for a bigger dealer in Oklahoma City. We would have people in and out - he would leave for hours and come back in the early hours of the morning on the weekends. He was not usually gone during the week.

He and his connection were close, and they had known each other for quite some time. He was having marital problems and had shown up at our house unannounced one afternoon. He had convinced my man that he should take off to Vegas with him to party for a few days.

He had plenty of marijuana, cocaine, and money! Of course, he was not going without me – I was so insecure I was not going to let him out of my sight. I was so jealous and worried he was going to cheat on me.

Mainly because his dealer had a reputation for cheating on his wife, and I was not sure if I could completely trust my man to say no in his friend's presence. So, we headed to Vegas.

First, we took my daughter to my mother's, and of course, the connection met my older sister. She couldn't resist a man with money and drugs and a free trip to Vegas! She ended up hooking up with the connection and joined us on the trip.

We never made it any further than the flight to Kansas City and the 5-star hotel we stayed the night in. His connection had a major cocaine habit. I'm not sure whether he shot it up, smoked it, or just snorted it, but he became extremely paranoid.

He kept my man in his room all night, and we ended up leaving the next morning for Oklahoma City via Greyhound bus. Around a week later, we received a phone call from his wife, informing us that authorities had found his body on a Florida beach. He had died of an overdose. We never found out if it was on purpose or an accident. It was not long after this trip that my mother threatened to take my daughter from me if a psychiatrist didn't see me.

She habitually used this threat constantly to keep me in line. I tried to use the threat of never seeing her granddaughter again to control things, but it rarely worked until I grew into my twenties and had the actual means to leave the house with my daughter and not have to bring her back for any reason.

I checked myself into the psychiatric ward at St. Anthony Hospital under the pressure of the psychiatrist, who told me that if I didn't check myself in voluntarily, he would commit me for 30 days.

I chose to check myself in so that I could check myself out at any time without anyone's permission or a court order. I had been diagnosed with severe depression. I was never diagnosed with anything other than depression.

All I did for two weeks was sit in a group of people and listen to them talk about their alcohol and drug addictions. I did not have an addiction problem. I was not addicted to cocaine. I had only done it for a few months; I was not addicted.

I had already walked away from it and given it up cold turkey a month before I checked myself in this place. The only drug addictions I had were nicotine and sugar. I made baskets and watched television. They only treated the symptoms of my depression. No one has ever treated the problem.

They just wanted to give me pills. I took the pills; I never felt any different – good or bad – just never felt anything.

I checked out of the hospital and grabbed a ride with a co-worker's husband. He picked me up, and we went to his house, where we had sex. I was experiencing another manic episode, engaging in highly risky behavior as I usually did. Despite feeling increasingly restless, I was eager to leave the hospital and return home. My mental and emotional health were not my priorities. I just wanted to move forward with life, find the next relationship or job, and ignore my depression. I tried to suppress these feelings.

This behavior was a downward spiral. I had quit my job and was trying to escape my relationship. I was avoiding my responsibilities. It felt like a call from a deeper part of myself, signaling my world was falling apart. This period marked the height of my darkest moments, urging me to stop avoiding my issues and start healing my inner wounds.

My daughter adored Stevie Nicks. I felt it was meant to be for her fourth birthday, coinciding with Ms. Nicks' concert for her "Wild Heart" album. I splurged on two front-row tickets with an entire paycheck. I had made a promise to my daughter to see her idol up close.

We dressed in our best outfits and found our seats, waiting through the opening act. My daughter grew impatient, constantly asking when Stevie would perform. It was well past her bedtime when Ms. Nicks finally appeared. Then, amidst the excitement, my daughter nearly got trampled. A security guard had noticed her early on, lifting her onto a chair behind a barrier for safety. Despite my warnings, she attempted to climb onto the stage.

I'm not sure of every detail, but suddenly, my daughter was off the chair and moving towards the stage. Stevie stopped her performance to pick up my daughter. Holding her, she resumed singing and danced with her, spinning around and kissing her cheek. My daughter was singing with her, and the smile on her face was incredible – she was just beaming! That was my daughter – my baby girl – OH MY GOD! Was this really happening? This was the moment of a lifetime!

It was an amazing night that I will never forget! On the drive home, she kept saying how she wanted to see her again and how good she smelled. Such a wonderful memory!

A small rock news publication circulated in our city back in the eighties when this concert took place, and a photograph of my daughter in Stevie's arms was on the paper's front page. The actual black-and-white photograph and newspaper article are in my daughter's possession.

It is an amazing experience that she will be able to share with her grandchildren and great-grandchildren! This will always be one of the major highlights of my life!

Chapter 6: Shifting Shadows

Over the years, I've realized it's all too easy to get used to our own pain. We get so wrapped up in all the wrongs and forget any rights, losing sight of better days if there ever were any. Hope dims, and the fear of change creeps in.

We settle into that fear, trying to make do with what life has handed us. But I've learned something important: those who dare to step beyond their suffering, seeking a higher purpose, are the ones who truly thrive.

Our struggles feel endless, piling up one after another, yet they're not permanent.

Constant? – Yes! Permanent? – No.

They only linger because we hold onto them. The moment we decide to let go and aim for a brighter existence, that's when we break free.The common denominator that attracted me to my love interests was usually some sort of drug or alcohol use. I didn't drink, but I did experiment with drugs. However, if I had a bad experience, I never did that drug again.

I tried quaaludes and cocaine and smoked tons of marijuana with this partner. I spent a month in a psychiatric ward by self-admittance, and he remained by my side. He was a good man, but I was so messed up emotionally and mentally I could not be faithful. I broke his heart and regret the way I treated him. I made bad decisions due to the trauma and emotional neglect that I had experienced in my childhood and young adulthood, as well as the mental abuse I had suffered. My mother never acknowledged my mental or emotional pain from the situations that created them, but she never acknowledged all that stemmed from the fallout of the aftermath that followed, either.

She did not prepare me for the extra burden of her guilt, shame, rage, depression, sadness, and self-loathing - all negative emotions or thoughts that stemmed from the situation - a thought, a feeling - anything - she laid it on me to carry for her. I carried that burden for her and myself for over forty-six years.

I've let that go and put it all to rest forever. Never to look upon it ever again. She is out of my life for good, and it feels good. Yes, it had been difficult to let go of that want for the mother I never had and will never have. Having to let go of the want, desire, and even need for validation from the mother that only existed in my mind.

The mother that never existed and will never exist in reality. That was the hardest part of letting go. Overcoming the idea, the thought you have of the mother you want her to be, and that you believe she can be and letting go of the hope that she can be that mother that you so desperately need her to be for you.

Realizing that she will never be that and you must let go, and in doing so, you may need to let her go too, especially if she is abusive and/or toxic to you or for you. When you realize that your own mother, the one that is supposed to protect and nurture you, left you vulnerable and alone to fight on your own for survival when you needed her most and holds a grudge against you for the very life that you live, it can be Soul crushing.

Discovering that you were the only "mistake" out of all her five children. Realizing that she blames you for her loneliness, the loss of the love of her life, the destruction of her marriage, the loss of her home, her status, her happiness, her future, and so on can be like a jolt of lightning to the core of your being.

I ran into my crush, I believe, at one of the bars that I started going to on occasion with a woman I had made friends with at the vo-tech I attended. He always had a way of drifting into and out of my life.

I was starting to grow apart from my partner, and every time I would see my crush, it would stir that old pull towards him I would feel but could not explain. This was a strange, inexplicable feeling of a Soulmate type of energy.

I'm sure I knew him from a past life. He was a past-life Soul connection, maybe even more than one past-life connection. We spent a couple of weeks together, going from hotel room to hotel room with another couple.

She was a dancer with a Chow-Chow dog, and her boyfriend was some bum whose name I cannot even remember. She had tattoos of her two dogs on her hip bones, one on each side. She owned a five-foot Boa snake that I took care of for a couple of weeks after we all stopped hanging out, but she struck the glass at my daughter, so I immediately took her to the apartment where the girl was staying.

During those couple of weeks, I really did not hear from her or my crush. After I delivered the snake, I did not hear from my crush for a few years. He disappeared like he always did. He would come into my world every few years, stir it up, pull me from a good relationship, steal from me, and then leave me broken-hearted. After the loss of his best friend, the time I spent with my crush, the time spent in the psych ward, and my bipolar outburst, co-dependent, and destructive behavior, I had grown bored and restless in my relationship and wanted something and someone new.

I went out dancing one evening with my girlfriend. I met my next partner at a club named Quicksilver's. He looked like Eddie Van Halen, and I was a huge Van Halen fan. I had seen him a couple of years earlier at a bar called After the Gold Rush when I was dating the Green Beret.

He had been married to his second wife back then. I had a fake ID and was sneaking into clubs to dance back in those days, and I had noticed them as a couple. She was very attractive, and he was as well. Little did I know back then that I would end up in his life.

My daughter was five years old when I met my son's father. He was standing at the bar ordering a Kamikaze when I walked by. I lightly touched his shoulder and asked for a light. That's how it started. He, of course, bought me a rose from the rose lady and brought it to my table. He was out with his friends; drinking, as I found out later, was a nightly habit, and they had had a bet going for a few weeks.

They bet on who could have sex with the most women in a row without being turned down. The way I understood it was he had approached twelve women so far, and he had slept with all of them. I was his thirteenth conquest, and I broke his streak because I went home. A few weeks later, we were renting a small house and moving in together. I broke one's heart to win another's. That was my MO with him and my last partner. Most of the time, a man would do something disrespectful to me or would make me question their loyalty, hurt my feelings, or break my trust – I'd lose love, respect, and/or trust for them, I would distance myself, and feel less for them – we, of course, would argue, nothing would be settled. I would become resentful and bitter. I would hold that against them.

They would do something else; I would distance myself further - the more negative they did, the more distant I would become - I would lose more interest in them – the more we would argue – the more I would shut down – I would distance myself more – I would find someone else and move on. This was the process MO.

This new man and I argued a lot about his best friends, whom he had known since junior high school, mainly because they would drink constantly and act like twelve-year-olds, breaking my things by roughhousing inside the house. Generally, all they did when they got together was drink. He was an alcoholic when I met him and up until he met his current wife.

When we met, he had his painting company. He had secured a contract for one of the larger apartment complexes in our small city, and when he needed some labor help because the client was not paying their invoices and could no longer make payroll, I went to work for him for free.

I would work with him during the day and then cook and take care of the home at night. I did this for quite some time. Things were going well, as we had other clients and were holding our own with just us as employees, so we decided to buy a home. It was not a good idea, but no one said we were smart or making good decisions, and we could never have predicted the future.

A year and a half into our relationship, my daughter's father decided he wanted custody of her. My ex-partner, hurt by my actions, agreed to help him. Unbeknownst to me, my sister was taking my daughter to see my ex, attempting to form a romantic bond with him while I was in a new relationship. During this time, my daughter's father and my ex were collecting information from my sister and family to use against me.

Surprisingly, my ex and I arrived together at his deposition, where he changed his statement, which led to the custody motion's dismissal. Without his testimony, they had no grounds to proceed. He admitted to drug use but protected my reputation, not disclosing any of my actions in front of my daughter or while she was in my care.

He knew that if her father gained custody, he wouldn't see her again. Despite the pain I caused him, he played a crucial role in maintaining custody of my daughter. We both understood the consequences if he had been truthful. I had prayed fervently to retain custody, and it felt like a higher power answered my prayers, guiding and protecting me, even from myself, throughout my challenges.

Yet, I remained oblivious to the guidance meant to set me on a better path, ignoring the signs urging me to heed the voice of the Divine. After securing my daughter's custody, we faced financial difficulties. Nine months after buying our home, he declared bankruptcy for his business, and we lost our house. We temporarily moved in with his parents, where the situation was far from welcoming. His mother disapproved of me, possibly preferring her son to be with someone of Asian descent. I was the third woman in his life, potentially his second wife, and being white and American made me particularly undesirable to her. She and her friends would often speak in their native language in my presence, undoubtedly to make me feel unwelcome, often discussing me, adding to the strain of an already challenging time.

One afternoon, she sparked an argument over something trivial and demanded that my daughter and I leave her house immediately. Her outrage was so intense that she went outside to wait for her husband, refusing to re-enter the home until he removed us. That night, I moved out with my daughter.

We stayed with my mother for a few days before moving into a small Oklahoma City school district rental house. I preferred not to have my daughter in that district, but I had no alternative at the time. The school wouldn't start for a few more months, giving me time to plan our next steps.

Unbeknownst to us, I became pregnant while we were staying at his parents' house. We were living in a small rental near my mother's home. My boyfriend struggled to find work in Oklahoma City; he hardly looked for a job. Following a hurricane, his best friend found out about construction opportunities in Galveston, Texas, and decided to head there. My boyfriend chose to follow, attracted by the potential earnings. He planned to work there and send money home, and if the job turned out to be stable, he would set up a home for us in Texas and call for us later.

However, we discovered the pregnancy just as he decided to leave. I felt insecure in our relationship due to his mother's interference, his unemployment, and his departure to Texas for an indefinite period. I didn't trust him or his friends. He sent me back to my mother's without assurance of his return. Consequently, we decided to terminate the pregnancy, a decision I regret now.

I believe he still resents me for it, nearly forty years later, blaming me as though I made the choice alone without his agreement. I try to convince myself that my son is the same Soul as the one we lost, but I remain uncertain. I sometimes think I should have been a mother to three. Yet, at the time, it seemed like the best decision.

Of course, there were no jobs in Texas. He just wanted to escape from the reality of losing his business and bankruptcy. The idea of working for someone else haunted him, although he pretended to search for employment. He indulged in uninterrupted fun with his two best buddies, experiencing a mid-life crisis in his early thirties. But when the money ran out, he came crawling home.

No job meant no future. I should have left then but wouldn't have had my son. We married soon after, struggling to make ends meet over the next year. He decided to return to school for business and photography. He believed he could make a living as a photographer with his nice cameras and darkroom equipment.

Though he was talented, he never earned a dime. He dreamed of shooting semi-nude and nude photographs for women's intimate gifts, using me as his model. Despite creating business cards and promotional materials, his venture went nowhere. Not one commercial booking came his way, except for a free shoot for his best friend's wife. When we divorced, he was supposed to return all the photographs and negatives he took of me, but I never received them, assuming they'd been destroyed.

I became pregnant with my son about a year into our marriage. My daughter was seven, and I desired another child, preferably a boy. He wasn't as enthusiastic, but he'd always longed for a son since his firstborn was a girl.

We resided in a rundown apartment complex, the Fleetwood Apartments, occupying a roach-infested one-bedroom unit where even the bugs seemed to mock us. The place was decrepit, with wooden floors, painted-shut windows, and rickety stairs. We lived in discomfort because he refused to work. Rent was $150 a month, including utilities, in 1986, when things were more affordable.

We were living on my measly $200.00 a month of child support from my daughter's father and what was left from Pell Grant and student loan money. I do not recall him working at that time except with his father. His father owned his own window-washing business for over 20 years.

The same customers the entire time he had the business. He may have even run the business after his father died. Most of them were in the small city next to ours. He did not make much, but it helped with expenses. We may have been using food stamps at the time, too. I cannot recall for sure, but we must have been in order to feed the three of us.

We moved into a house before my son was born. My pregnancy with my son was not as difficult as my pregnancy with my daughter. I was not bedridden, but I did have high blood pressure and preeclampsia, just not as severe. I could not wear shoes, my ankles were so swollen, and I only had one dress and one pantsuit that I could wear because I had no maternity clothes. I was denied sexual contact throughout my pregnancy; my husband refused to have sex with me, and I had to beg for it. He wanted nothing to do with a "fat" woman.

Once I lost weight, he wanted to have sex with me, but while I was heavy with child, he rejected me. I never forgave him for that. That's one of the reasons why I had an affair after my son was born, and I was no longer in love with my husband because of the way he made me feel about myself when I was pregnant and how he treated me then. My lover found me attractive when I had some weight on my body after my son was born and then after I lost weight.

My daughter was one day shy of being nine months to the day of her due date, and she was due September 18th. My son was two days overdue from his due date; he was due July 7th. I wanted to induce labor or take him by c-section. The doctors wanted to ensure that his lungs were developed enough before making any decision, so they wanted to do an amniocentesis.

Now, we did not know the sex of the baby at the time, and back then, it was rare, if not unheard of, to find out the sex of the baby before it was born because you had to pay for it out of your own pocket when the state was paying your medical treatment.

After the procedure, the doctor informed us that his lungs had developed enough, and everything was good. I could be induced, or we could set a date for c-section delivery. The doctor asked us if we wanted to know the sex of the baby. We absolutely did!

When he announced that it was a boy, my husband was so overjoyed he almost left me behind in the hospital; he was so anxious to get to the car so he could go tell everyone he was having a son. I was waddling as fast as I could go to keep up.

I was so elated! I was going to have my boy! I had a girl, and now I had my boy; everything was perfect!

We set a date to induce labor. I went into labor that night, though, as one of the risks of the procedure I had that day was it could send you into labor.

My son's birth was somewhat uneventful. The only thing that stands out is the fact that I was not advancing in dilation with my contractions, and I was sleeping through them. The head of OB came in and asked me how I wanted to have the baby. Did I want to have him vaginally or by c-section?

I chose c-section because I was having my tubes tied anyway. So, we proceeded with his birth. This c-section was easy as pie! I knew what was coming and was not so panicked and/or afraid. None of my family or my husband's family were there for his birth. I believe everyone bombarded me for the next two days. I was at the hospital and at home with visits, and no one called first.

My son was so small he could fit in a shoe box and had a head full of black hair. His little feet were as small as his father's index finger. So tiny.

The difficult times were the first year of my son's life. The colic was the worst! His father was excited at first; having a son was great. He had finally one-upped his best friend. His best friend had him beaten by his looks, the women he had been with, the money he had, etc. His friend always outdid him; he was always better. Not this time!

His best friend only had daughters. But he had a son. Proud wasn't a big enough word to describe how he felt. He could not get enough of him! Until the colic set in. The hours of crying, night after night – that lasted for about three months. Walking, bouncing over the knees, patting the back. He did not have any more patience than I did.

He would get so frustrated. I handled it most of the time because he could not handle it. He would often get angry and yell. He would take it out on me and my daughter. There were different rules for each child. We did not use corporal punishment on our son, but he used it on my daughter.

My husband did not like my mother, and she did not care for him either. He seldom allowed her or my family to be around my son. As a result, my son hardly knows my mother or my family. He has seen them only a few times throughout his life. From the age of seventeen to now, he has seen me maybe ten or twenty times. We are not close and likely never will be. I feel we have been estranged for the better part of his life, more by his choice than mine. I continued to pay child support despite our agreement that I wouldn't need to. Yet, I didn't see him from the ages of twelve to seventeen. This distance has always been his choice once he was old enough to decide for himself.

His father's parents adored my son. He was the grandchild they felt closest to. Their other grandchildren lived in the northern part of the state. During our marriage, I only met his oldest brother and his family once. We visited their home. His father and I got along well until our marriage ended. His mother could not stand me.

I did not know his oldest brother well enough to gauge his feelings towards me. He had another older brother, between him and the eldest, who was disabled and with whom I had no interaction. The story goes that his disability resulted from a flu shot his mother received while pregnant. That's all the explanation I received. This brother spent his days in his room, wandering the house at night. After their parents passed, the eldest brother took him in.

Doctors advise that after a C-section, you shouldn't lift anything heavier than your baby (7 lbs. 5 oz.) for the first two weeks. When I returned from the hospital, I found a dirty house, piles of laundry, and many dishes to wash. He hadn't cleaned at all during my three-day absence. This situation mirrored our entire relationship: I did everything, carrying both the feminine and masculine burdens. This pattern repeated in all my relationships. I gave my all and received nothing in return.

We went through the same argument time and again. I was doing everything. He wouldn't hold down a job or help with the children or household duties. To be clear, he was lazy. I realized the only way I'd achieve anything material was on my own. This wasn't the man I was meant to spend my life with. By then, my son was about a year old.

His best friend decided to take CDL classes to hit the open road and make a fortune. He planned to retire in his fifties. My husband believed he would also make a vast amount of money driving trucks, setting himself up for life in just a few years. He always thought he'd strike it rich, regardless of the plan, but never had the motivation to follow through.

I managed everything at home while he went to trucking school and then worked as a truck driver. It was tough. The pay was low, and he was hardly home, creating the perfect storm. The money he earned was spent on his living expenses on the road, leaving nothing for us. He failed to provide. Given our already unstable foundation, I had warned him our marriage couldn't withstand his job choice. Yet, he didn't listen. The first three months, with no earnings, should have been a sign, but it took him over a year to realize that he had lost nearly everything.

I decided to study floral design for a steady income, assuming flowers are always in demand. When I chose to go back to school and work, he suddenly left trucking for a "real" job. It seemed my independence threatened his control. He couldn't stand not knowing my whereabouts every minute of the day, me earning my own money, or becoming my own person.

I started school, and he found a job on the midnight shift painting planes at the Air Force base. I attended school until 3:00 p.m. while my daughter cared for her little brother during my classes and while my husband slept. He would leave for work as I returned home, ensuring the children were never alone. After graduating and starting work, I saved money and planned to leave my husband, intending to take both children with me. However, my husband forcibly took my son and refused to return him. Unable to physically retrieve my son without causing harm and lacking a court order, I left without him. My husband thought holding my son would force me to return, but I didn't. His plan failed.

I never went back. He blamed me for his having to raise a child he didn't want on his own out of spite and made me suffer for it. He told my son I had abandoned him, though, in reality, I left his father, not him. His father used him to manipulate me, but I never had the chance to explain this to my son, who will never know the truth.

After waiting five years for him to get a regular job and put his life together, I had enough. I had an affair while he was away driving trucks, something I had warned would ruin our marriage, but he didn't listen. He followed his friend into trucking without considering the consequences. Though he eventually got a decent job, I left him.

He lost that job soon after. He ended up unemployed, with a new car that was stolen and stripped after moving back to Fleetwood Apartments. He raised my son in terrible conditions but still wouldn't let me take him. He preferred having him in a roach, rat-infested apartment than a clean, secure home. He resented the court-ordered weekends my son spent with me and made things difficult by not providing necessities despite knowing I was struggling too.

I set up my home with just my daughter and myself for the first time when she was ten, and I was twenty-seven years old. I had spent years answering to someone and living my life as someone else wanted. I was finally free to do as I pleased. I had no mother or man controlling me—I was finally free. We didn't have much, but we were happy.

That changed when I started partying too much. I worked but partied on the weekends. Friday and Saturday nights were lit!! I don't know how I managed to stay alive. My routine was grueling. Up at 5:00 a.m. on Friday for work, then after an eight-hour shift, I'd come home at 5:30 p.m., shower, do my make-up and hair, and be ready by 8:00 p.m. to club until 2:00 a.m., followed by breakfast until 4:00 a.m. We didn't get home until 5:00 a.m., slept until 10:00 a.m., then cleaned the house and did laundry. By 4:00 p.m., we'd start getting ready again to arrive at the club by 7:00 p.m., securing a good table by the dance floor to watch all the men come in. We'd dance until close, then it was breakfast until 4:00 a.m., home by 5:00 a.m., and sleep until 11:00 a.m., trying not to mess up our normal sleep schedule. If it were a three-day weekend, we'd do this on Sunday too! Come Monday, it was back to the grind.

My daughter was scheduled to spend that first Christmas with her father. My son's father and I had only been separated a few months and were not on good terms, so my son spent all the holidays that year with his father. I had no money for a tree or presents anyway, so not being with my children for the holidays was not as devastating as he had hoped. Don't get me wrong, it was killing me to be away from them, especially my son, that Christmas, but I wasn't going to let him know that.

I went to Albuquerque, New Mexico, with one of the directors from the vo-tech I had attended that Christmas. It was a tough holiday to get through and not the best trip, but I wanted to get as far away from home as possible to distract myself from what was happening. I didn't want to sit in my little house alone.

I'll never forget that holiday. It was supposed to be in the forties and fifties with snow, but it ended up being in the seventies, and we were up in the mountains with no snow.

However, the town was beautiful, with lights in little brown paper bags lining the streets and sidewalks through the neighborhoods all the way up the mountain.

I attended midnight mass at a lovely little Catholic church with the family I was staying with. Despite missing my children, I appreciated not being alone. This trip was another opportunity to heed the call of my Higher Self, presented during the service at that little church in Albuquerque. Since that divorce, I've spent more time alone and have had more chances to respond to the call of my Higher Self than I care to admit.

I did not do anything but work and party for the next three years. On the weekends, I had my kids; I tried to stay home. I spent the days with them, but some nights, I left my son with my daughter and hit the town. Most times at the club, ladies got in free, or there was a $2.00 cover charge. I did not have money for activities like waterparks or the zoo with my children. I barely had gas money to get to work and rarely had a working car. My daughter was on the free breakfast and free lunch program at school. We didn't have a television and listened to music all the time. I usually didn't have money for groceries, so we ate fast food a lot when we did eat. Things were tough, and children don't seem to remember these struggles when they grow up. They want to punish, guilt, and shame you for being a horrible parent. I did my best to provide. I will admit I was not the best parent, but I wasn't born into the best of circumstances myself. I wasn't focused on bettering myself or my situation; I was just trying to survive. Survival was all I knew.

I tried to be there for my children emotionally, physically, financially, and mentally. I ensured they had clean clothes and were clean, and their basic needs were met. I made sure to let them know that I was proud of them at every opportunity. I always told them that I may not have approved of what they did, but I would always love them. I missed a lot of their childhood because I was always working and couldn't take off to go to their plays, ball games, or other events. Someone had to support the family: when we were a family, when it was just my daughter and me when it was me and my freeloading husbands, and myself when there was no one else.

I was hard on my daughter about making good grades and doing chores, which included dishes, maybe taking out the trash, and cleaning her room. I did everything else: the laundry, mopping, vacuuming the floors, cleaning the bathrooms—all the heavy lifting. My mother made me do everything. That is how I knew how to do everything. But in other ways, I was very lenient.

I was not allowed to have friends over, but she was.

I was not permitted to spend the night with someone, nor were they allowed to spend it with me, but she was allowed on both counts.

I couldn't talk to boys or have them over, but she could. I wasn't allowed phone calls, but she was. She could pick out her clothes and do her own hair. She was told she was pretty, smart, funny, and that I was proud of her. She was assured she could do anything she put her mind to and that I loved her no matter what she said or did. I was never allowed to do or had never heard these affirmations.

I validated her as much as I could. I never called her names or told her she was worthless. I never told her she wasn't worth the dynamite it would take to blow her ass to hell! I never said anything like that to her, yet I heard such things more than once in my childhood.

My neglect was a form of abuse; it took its toll on my daughter, and she lashed out. The one time I loosened the reins and let her go somewhere without parental supervision, she lied about going to the state fair. Instead, she spent the day running around town with her friends, causing turmoil and stealing candy from school property. This got her arrested.

I received a call from the local police department. My daughter could not have been more upset and sorry for what she had done. She was upset that she got caught—that was the issue. I was at my wits' end. She was slowly becoming delinquent and had never been so defiant before.

This issue had begun several months prior (I later learned that she had lost her virginity at the age of twelve, behind a church, and that she had secretly gone swimming at night at Lake Draper, which is specifically a drinking water lake with absolutely NO SWIMMING; I nailed her windows shut to prevent this from happening again), and it had gotten worse over time. She was spoiled rotten. She had gotten pretty much what she wanted because she had been a good kid and an only child for so long before her brother was born. She loved school, was a good student, and a great little athlete—she played t-ball as a small child and then softball for her grandfather's ball teams. I had never had this kind of trouble out of her, but suddenly, at twelve/thirteen years old, she was becoming a problem—and fast.

Little did I know at the time that her father had broken apart her relationship between her and her grandfather—the only father figure she had ever known. She was lashing out, and I did not realize it. She was crying for help, but she never came to me. She never said she needed to talk, nothing.

She and I were arguing about the situation the next day, and we almost came to blows. If my co-worker, Janet (I called her Janet from another planet), who had lived with us for a little while, had not stepped in between us, there would have been a fistfight in the middle of that living room. But because she stepped between us, my daughter has been disrespectful to me from that day forward.

I never put her in her place when she called me a bitch, and so she has always threatened to hurt me physically and has bullied me since that day. I sent her to her father's home for two weeks for him to straighten her out, but her defiance only worsened, and she turned into a bossy bully and still is to this day.

At the end of those two weeks, she decided she wanted to stay with her father because he could offer her so much more financially and materialistically. Clothes, tennis clubs, cheerleading camps, fastpitch teams, popularity in school—all things I could not give her because I did not make her father's money since he had a job at TAFB. I cried, listening to her say those words. Listening to her tell me I was not a good parent, that I could not provide her with what she needed or wanted.

Those words killed me.

To this day, she does not recognize the pain and the heartache those words caused me. I suppose we all forget the pain we have inflicted and only remember the pain we received. I have learned from completing my Karmic Cycles the pain from both sides.

You cannot heal until you understand both positions. You must connect with both the pain you received from others and the pain you have given to others before you can truly connect with your Higher Self and heal the Inner Child because the pain you have given is the reflection of the pain you have received.

Physical abuse was a form of discipline that I was taught to use to force children to comply. I was not exposed to any other forms of discipline or processes for handling situations with a small child, either in trouble or creating a scene in public. Gentle parenting did not exist in my mother's time, and she did not pass it along to me. My mother's method was to snatch you up and tear into you, regardless of the setting. So, forgive me for my ignorance. Children, especially, mimic what they see, being led by example. I didn't have a good parental model, so a bit of forgiveness is in order. I should, you might say, forgive my mother for her actions based on the example she was given, and so on. I have recently discovered a philosophy stating that forgiveness is not necessary for healing. I'm not quite sure where I stand on this issue. I am grateful for the lessons I learned from my mother. A year ago, I couldn't have said this. By not embodying these qualities, she inadvertently taught me to be loving, compassionate, empathetic, gentle, and kind. I am also grateful for the lessons I will discover from my father, whatever those may be.

The lessons from people I have encountered and will encounter are valuable, too. Each event in our lives, minor or major, teaches us something. As you move through your Spiritual Awakening Journey, you learn to appreciate these lessons. They raise your consciousness, bringing you closer to healing your Inner Child, integrating the Higher Self, Inner Child, and Shadow Self, and connecting you to the Divine. The true path to healing involves using trauma and negative experiences as lessons, drawing something positive from them. This positive lesson and the energy it brings empowers you to make positive changes in yourself, which then reflects onto the collective and spreads across nations.

My daughter's resentment towards me stems from the fact that I abused her when she was young. I sent her to her father's home at thirteen (for disciplinary reasons, and she chose to stay), and I allowed my son's father to spank her with a large wooden paddle—yes, it was abusive. I have acknowledged, owned, and apologized for all of these things many times, yet she still holds a grudge against me. I have done all I could do to make amends. Nothing seems to satisfy her need to inflict guilt and shame on our past. I have learned my lessons from this relationship as well. My mistakes and the things I did incorrectly. I did the best I could with the examples I was given, the emotional and mental capacities I had at the time, my financial capabilities at the time, and my lack of self-control. I have accepted my truth, and I hope she does as well someday.

My son resents me because he feels he has been abandoned by me twice. Once, I left his father when he was two and a half years old, and once when he was twelve, and I did not choose him over my husband at the time. He has told me he has "forgiven" me, but what do I need to be forgiven for, I ask you? I left his father, not him, and he chose to stop seeing me when he was twelve. I did not tell him I did not want to see him anymore.

He told me in his mid-twenties straight to my face that he did not have time for me, and I hadn't seen him for three years or more. I mourned over my son's decision for years; there are times I still mourn him (and both my children) as if they have passed.

As I have said, I did the best I could. I admit I made mistakes, but I do not know one parent who hasn't. It's just that some of us make bigger ones than others. I have stopped picking up the guilt from all the transference from my mother, daughter, and son. I no longer carry guilt of any kind. I have completed my Karmic Cycle; my Karma was the separation from my children. They have chosen no contact; therefore, my Karmic Cycle has been completed.

During that time of discovery, I will not deny I was promiscuous and wild. I spent my free time at the clubs - dancing and socializing. Making up for the years I missed in my youth because I had a child so young, I had no friends – I was finally attractive – men looked at me, and I was enjoying it. I did not drink alcohol, so I was always the designated driver. I had a rule that if you rode with me to the club, you left the club with me. If you met someone, they could meet you wherever we were having breakfast and then follow you home. But you were riding home with me. I made sure you made it home, inside your house, before I left you.

That way, I could honestly tell the authorities that I left you safe and sound at home. Of course, I did not realize it then, but the only "friends" I had were those who rode with me every weekend to the club. They were only around when it was time to grab a ride to the club. I was being used but did not realize it then because I was desperate for "friends."

I brought more than my share of men home. Sometimes, on the nights, my kids were at home. This was my entire social life. These were my "friends." The people, I thought, cared about me. Little did I know they were just using me for rides and a place to crash when they were between places to stay. I was in my prime. I was in my late twenties, headed into my thirties.

Life was just starting.

I was starting to make my way and set my own rules. I had a steady job, was making what, at the time, was considered decent money for a single woman, and had a running car and a house.

We were barely getting by, but we were making it. I saw my son every other weekend, and things had settled into somewhat of a routine, and life was moving right along.

Chapter 7: Emergence

One afternoon, I had returned from a run to the grocery store and was headed into the house when a car pulled up. A guy yelled out my name from the driver's side. I did not recognize him or the car. I was a bit scared, wondering if some weirdo had followed me home from the club or if I had given my number to some guy I did not remember. Who was this guy? He had to tell me who he was.

Holy shit! It was my crush! I had not seen him in at least six years. He was standing in my yard, just as clear as day! There he stood in all his glory. He had not changed much, just a little older. He was not as handsome as I remembered; you could tell the years hadn't been very kind, but I still felt that little jolt in my chest when I realized who he was. He had seen me in the grocery store and followed me home a few weeks earlier but did not have the nerve to stop and say hello.

He saw me today and could not resist saying something. He lived in the neighborhood and wanted to know how I was doing. I invited him in to catch up.

He had been in prison for the past five years or so (for several felonies, I found out later). I was unsurprised; he and his brothers were known for their troubled pasts, always in trouble with the law. That's one of the main reasons my mother didn't like their kind. His brother (before he died) and my sister, who were involved, kept us apart fifteen years ago. Despite this, we both felt the pull toward each other. It was obviously there, or he would not have followed me through the grocery store and all the way home a week ago and then stopped by today. I was elated to see him and hopeful that we could have the relationship we were denied in our youth. Little did I know I would learn the hard lesson of being careful about what you wish for because you might just get it. It was not long before he was in my bed. One evening, after being intimate, I asked him nonchalantly what he was thinking, and out of nowhere, he said, "I love you."

I about fell out of bed! Here was my crush, of ALL people, tough guy reputation – had been with his daughter's mother, his "wife" of twelve years, and he is telling me he loves me and is saying it first? Shock, complete shock.

During the time of kindling the relationship with my crush, he was still married (although common law) and living with her and his daughter; I was still seeing other men (for a while). I saw several married men while I was a single woman. It was more convenient for me. No attachments. I could do as I pleased, but they could not hold me to any rules, regulations, or obligations and vice versa. It worked out perfectly.

Except for my crush. That's where things were complicated because I was "in love" with him. I had carried a torch for him since I was fourteen years old, and he was my "Soulmate." I was willing to break up a family or whatever else I had to do to have him. He was mine; I had waited all my life to have him, and I was not going to back down. I was going to do whatever it took. If it meant waiting forever, then so be it!! Geez, what an idiot!!! I was my mother personified!!! I did not see it then, but I can look back and see it now! He was a cheater! A liar! He could not be trusted. He had proven that to me several times when I was younger. He told me he would pick me up after school, give me a ride home, and then stand me up, and I had to walk miles home. The times he had come in and out of my life left me heartbroken. I had already experienced his past behavior; why did I think anything had changed?

All the days and nights sitting by the phone, not going out because I was afraid of missing his call or missing him if he stopped by and I was not there. Paging him over and over, and no response for days, weeks, and even months with no contact. Then he would show up, and I would drop everything for him. I'd see him for two or three days and then back to the old pattern.

I was his mistress for about seven years, never thinking I deserved more than that. Just being happy having him in my life, thinking that was enough, then realizing it wasn't. This behavior and acceptance of this behavior and treatment stemmed from my co-dependency, low self-esteem, low self-confidence, and low self-worth.

Eventually, I reached a breaking point and demanded he pick me or her. He packed a sack of clothes and a few toiletry items and showed up at my apartment that Christmas. He stayed a few hours and left. He did not come back that night, and I didn't hear from him for a few weeks. He played tag, back and forth between her and me, for about a year or more before he finally made the big leap and left her for good.

When he finally decided, we moved into a small home on the city's north side. He was unhappy, and his attitude showed it. He missed his daughter, and I knew it. I am sure he was spending time with her every day he could, and if he was spending time with her, his "ex" was there, so inevitably, he was spending time with her, too. We started to build our life together. We argued like most couples, but this was always over his ex-wife. She was stalking me. I would see her sitting outside the house, watching me come and go. She made sure she was gone when he was home. I got tired of it, so one time, I called the police officers on her. I had warned him to tell her to stop doing it and that I would call the law on her if she did not stop it.

Well, I called them; they caught her pulling away from the curb and pulled her over. She had no license or insurance verification, and the tag on the car was expired, so they took her to jail. She spent the night there. His daughter called, all upset and crying. Her mother had used her phone call to call their daughter, so she called her father to get her out of jail.

I told him not to bail her out and that she needed to learn her lesson. He was furious because his daughter was so upset. I told him I had warned them and that she deserved what she deserved. He went and spent the night with his sixteen-year-old daughter because she was afraid to stay alone. She never messed with me again. I suppose this is why the family hated me so much.

At this time, he was working for a lawn service company and got injured on the job while planting a tree, requiring back surgery. He struggled with the pain post-surgery, even on a morphine drip. Demanding more potent "drugs" (his exact word), he threatened to obtain them from outside the hospital if the doctor wouldn't provide them. Consequently, they discharged him a few hours later, and the doctor terminated his care. He constantly complained that his pain medication wasn't strong enough. I tried to explain the importance of experiencing some pain to gauge his recovery process. However, a person craving drugs doesn't heed such advice. After a few days on Lortabs, I sent him a spiral. He couldn't satisfy his craving fast enough. Before long, he reverted to shooting up eight balls and falsely accused me of stealing his drugs. I would find him lying on the floor beside our bed at night, accusing me of inappropriate behavior in my sleep. His addiction had escalated to the point where he tore apart couch cushions, searching for drugs he believed were hidden or lost within.

I was the sole earner then, as his workers' compensation was dwindling. We moved to a cheaper house on the south side of town to escape our current living situation for something more affordable and to distance us from his ex-wife's prying eyes.

Conveniently for him, this area was closer to his dealer, facilitating his drug habit. That summer, amidst a record-breaking heat wave and without any air conditioning in our small home, he resorted to dousing the house's exterior with water late at night in an attempt to cool it down—a logic only an addict could rationalize.

It was a small two-bedroom house full of our furniture and boxes of belongings, mostly stacked in the spare room. There was no room to breathe, let alone live. I don't recall unpacking any boxes, sitting in the living room, watching television, or anything of that sort. All I really remember is the house being small, cramped and painted white with blue trim, and trying to sleep in it during the extreme heat.

My makeup vanity, boxes, and spare furniture were all crammed into that spare room. There was barely any room to access the closet for my clothes. I have OCD and cannot handle being in cluttered rooms or hoarding situations for more than a few minutes at a time. This house felt so small; it seemed like the walls were closing in on me. I felt trapped!!

I remember sitting at my makeup vanity, applying makeup in a room full of boxes and furniture, with him leaning on the door frame, complaining about something while I was trying to get ready for work. I remember seeing him standing outside in the backyard, smoking a cigarette under the streetlamp at the corner of the yard, making him look like a shadow just on the outskirts of the tree branches, hosing down the house in the summer heat.

I can't recall if his dealer got sick around this time, but he was home at night more often than usual, spending a lot of time hosing down the house after dark that summer. I couldn't handle the living situation, his drug problem, and the fact that I was supporting both of us, so I left him. I yearned for a new life: fresh, clean – no drugs. I felt like my life had become dirty, muddy, and covered in black soot. I wanted to wash it away – to cleanse it, to make it shiny, fresh, and new. Like in my past, I wanted to run, even from my Soulmate. I had grown tired of him and the situation and wanted out!

I was heading back to the north side of the city and began looking for a new job. I was determined to make a clean break. I wanted to elevate my self-esteem, believe I deserved better, and improve my materialistic status. I picked up one of those "apartments for rent" advertisement books and started searching for an apartment within my budget. The apartments I looked at offered all the amenities; I was set on getting the most for my money. I aspired to live as well as I knew I deserved, but I was unwilling to settle for less because I was burdened by supporting someone else and covering everyone else's bills. I found a nice apartment equipped with a washer and dryer, which meant no more trips to the laundromat. After paying the deposit and the first month's rent, I began moving in boxes and planned to arrange the transportation of my furniture. I was truly excited about my new beginning, but he followed me to my new place. He couldn't manage independently, and knowing how easily I could be manipulated, he convinced me to let him stay.

One Sunday morning, he left early, which wasn't unusual, and returned in the afternoon. He had gone to church that morning and spent time with the Pastor. He came back with a new perspective, having gotten clean with the Pastor's help, and urged me to join him at church. He then declared we couldn't live "in sin" any longer; we had to get married or live apart. There was my chance to leave, but foolishly, I missed it. I should have let him go, sparing myself a lot of heartache.

Our communication issues persisted; he still needed to finalize his divorce (back then, common law marriage was recognized in our state, requiring a legal divorce), and we were far from ready to marry, especially him—he was definitely not prepared!

He did not propose to me officially. One day, he was on a tangent and angry with me. He had come to my job to pick me up for lunch, and we had an argument. He threw the ring at me and said, "Here, that was going to be your engagement ring if you want it." I picked the ring up from off the floorboard of the truck and got out without saying a word, so I never really said yes. Our relationship was so rocky I should have known it wasn't right for me. It felt like some trauma bond. Maybe he was one of my

Soulmates? I'm not sure, but we were connected somehow. It was an extraordinarily strong bond. For a few years after our divorce, I would get calls from an "unknown" number, which I always thought was him trying to check up on me. Occasionally, one of his brothers would contact me through Facebook to ask how I was. But I have not heard from anyone in a very long time.

Our wedding was held in May 1999, the same year as the huge tornado. It hit on May 3rd, and we married on May 26th. He made extra money that year cleaning up storm-damaged properties, and we used that money for the wedding and our honeymoon in San Antonio. That trip was great.

It was my first vacation, and I thoroughly enjoyed it. I had a wedding dress, flowers, and my hair and nails professionally done—the works. I wanted a real wedding, and I made sure of it. My twelve-year-old son in a tuxedo with tails gave me away. My daughter was my bridesmaid, and she was higher than a kite in church, which I could not believe!

Our wedding day was great at the time. It wasn't a garage wedding or a justice of the peace ceremony. I was marrying the man of my dreams, my Soulmate (or so I thought), in a church, just as I had always dreamt. I didn't know that he had spent the night before with his ex-wife. I was unaware of the betrayal that had been ongoing the entire time we were together; nothing ever changed. He had never stopped seeing his ex-wife. He was still living two lives. We had joined his Free Methodist church when he decided to get clean and marry me. We had been baptized there and had been attending for about a year or so.

We did not have the reception I had dreamed of because it was at the church, with no dancing, no drinking—none of that. I am sure I hurt my family's feelings because I left with my husband's family not long after the service, and we went to Denny's for dinner to celebrate. I entered his family that day and exited mine. His family never accepted me, especially his mother.

She was close to his ex-wife, who had lived with them for most of their married life. She had to move out before they split up, and she knew that was the reason my ex-husband was kicking her out. He was preparing for his exit from the home, and she was unhappy because she had to find some way to support herself and make her own way. She had not worked her whole life; she had lived off the system and wasn't about to start now.

His mother did not like my older sister when she was married to his older brother because they had a lot of bad blood and dark water under the bridge. That gave her one more reason not to like me. I had broken the heart of her favorite daughter-in-law, and she shared in the hatred she had for me. I had destroyed her granddaughter's perfect life (even though her father was gone all the time to my house running around on her mom, and she knew it) and broke her little heart. Never mind, her son had done the same damn thing to them both. His daughter and mother were miserable at the wedding, but throughout the six years we were married.

The first four years of our marriage were not bad. We struggled with acceptance from his daughter and his mother. His daughter hated me passionately because her mother and grandmother hated me. I had "stolen" her father from her mother. She never blamed her father for his feelings for me but blamed me for my feelings for her father. We were productive and active members of the church for six years. My daughter was married (her first marriage), my son was baptized, and my granddaughter was Christened in that church; it was family to us. I was extremely happy and at peace during this time. I had come to terms with my emotional and mental trauma involving my father and had forgiven him. I had found peace with that situation and was finding my place among the women of the church, finding my Soul sisterhood, if you will.

I had become comfortable and found my self-confidence singing on the praise and worship team. I sang in the women's choir, Joyful Song, and performed solos during church service. I was performing "Ava Maria," a cappella in Latin, at Christmas services, which became a tradition for the Pastor every year. I was praying with one of my closest female parishioners every morning at 6:00 a.m. I went to bible study every Sunday and church services on Sundays and Wednesdays. I was following the organized religion's rules, standards, and morals. I had grown close to the Divine and thought I was finding my purpose. But unfortunately, it did not last.

We began having problems in our marriage around the beginning of the fifth year. I knew we were struggling a bit, but I did not think we were having any significant difficulties.

I started counseling with the junior female Pastor, who had once been a co-worker and whom I had known for about ten years. I had arrived for my weekly Tuesday night counseling session with Pastor. Our session hadn't been going long when we were interrupted by the senior Pastor, who requested that I come to his office to speak with him and my husband. I found it strange that the Pastor would want to talk to me with my husband present. What could be so serious that my husband needed to have the Pastor present?

All I could think was that my husband had committed adultery and wanted to tell me in front of the Pastor to prevent me from losing my senses, or he was back on drugs; it had to be something extremely serious. Then, remembering he had been ill recently and had been to the doctor, I braced myself for a cancer diagnosis.

I walked into the Pastor's office, and he asked me to take a seat. Looking at him and then at my husband, I said I would rather stand. However, he sternly told me I needed to sit down. He instructed my husband to speak, and my husband began to cry. I moved out of my chair and knelt down in front of him, telling him it was okay, that I loved him, and that everything would be alright; he just needed to tell me what was wrong.

Pastor came over and placed a hand on his shoulder, causing him to cry harder. I stood up and crossed my arms, bracing myself for him to say he had an affair. But what he said next completely floored me. Speaking through tears, he almost whispered, "I have HIV." My mind went blank; then my thoughts started racing—I couldn't stop or even slow them down. So many questions, so many emotions surfaced. All I could think to do was comfort HIM, make HIM feel better. Then, suddenly, the thought hit me – DO I HAVE IT????? I told him that I had married him until death do we part and that I meant those words. I would stay with him and take care of him when the time came. He never shared his true feelings or fears regarding his diagnosis, and I never asked. We never shared our deepest feelings; we did not have that type of relationship. Hell, I have never had that type of relationship with anyone. I tried my best to reassure him how much I cared for him. By this time, after everything that had happened in our relationship, I was unsure if I loved him. I felt bad for him, but part of me did not want to be with him anymore. He was terminally ill with a deadly disease. He could live twenty more years, or he could die in six months. He seemed to be pulling away from me more and more every day. It is like he wasn't interested in holding on to our relationship anyway. Like he was giving up, he worked and went about life, but he was just existing.

We never discussed the diagnosis, the treatment, or anything. All he was concerned about during any conversation was getting me tested. We had spent thirteen years together; I spent seven as his mistress and five as his legal wife. I was doing my best to help him want to hold onto life and choose to make the right health choices to survive and not have the disease develop into AIDS.

I'm not sure what was going through his mind; as I said, he didn't share his thoughts about his diagnosis or how he wanted to handle the future with me. I did research; I checked what I could do as far as sexual intimacy and such because they were still researching and learning things every day about the disease. We were told that the only way he could get his medication and treatment paid for was if we were not married. He decided on his own that two weeks after we celebrated our sixth-year wedding anniversary, he wanted me out of the house by mid-June and that he did not love me anymore. I knew things between us had gotten strained, and he had gotten distant, but I did not know it had gotten that bad. He did not explain, and he didn't want to talk about it. He just wanted me gone as soon as possible. I told him I needed thirty days. I needed at least two paychecks for the deposit and the first month's rent. I was out of the house, opened a new checking account (which he threw a fit about when he tried to withdraw my paycheck out of the joint account and there was no money in it – I knew what kind of thief he was, and I was one step ahead of him), filed for bankruptcy, had repossessed his new truck (which he couldn't understand why I would re-up on my car and not continue to pay for his too after he kicked me out of his life?); filed for divorce by the end of July and was legally divorced by September. The bankruptcy was finalized in February of the next year.

I do not fuck around; if you want me out of your life, I'm the fuck out - whether I'm heartbroken for years over you or not!! The last argument we had, I told him I would never marry again and would never have another relationship. I have found this to be true for sixteen years.

Before the diagnosis, my husband had picked up the job of custodian at the church when the gentleman who had been doing it decided to retire. He was trusted with the keys to the church, the church credit card, authorization to use the church's Home Depot account, and petty cash for cleaning and maintenance supplies. He also did minor lawn care and performed ice removal in the winter.

This worked out great for everyone; small maintenance jobs could be taken care of, the church was kept clean, and it supplemented our income during the winter months, especially since my husband only had a small lawn care business and did not work during winter.

He mowed our landlord's personal residential lawn and a couple of rental properties to pay our rent each month except during the winter; I made that up out of my paychecks, which caused a real hardship during that time of year. The other utilities and expenses were paid out of my checks year-round.

It was discovered that after our divorce, he was stealing from the church to pay for expenses for his lawn care business, and he was using the credit card to buy construction tools and reselling them for drug money because he had started doing drugs again after he kicked me out of the house, and I started the divorce process. The church had let him go without pressing charges.

When I found out what he had been doing, I never went back to church out of embarrassment. I know I did not do anything wrong, but the association was embarrassing. I occasionally see a woman I went to school with from the church at the bank. She's always kind; she always has been. We visit, but it is not the same; I am still uncomfortable around her. I lost a lot of knick-knacks, miniatures, clothes, and irreplaceable items when I moved from that house. I moved to a little one-bedroom apartment and did not have the room for all my things and didn't have the money for a storage unit. So, I lost most of the belongings that I had collected and accumulated over my lifetime.

He, of course, sold or pawned all the antiques and things that were worth any money to buy drugs and the rest he traded for drugs. There was an elderly woman from the church congregation that he helped who was homebound. She trusted him to write her checks to pay her bills. In fact, he may have even had his name on her checking account, and she trusted him like a son. I do believe he ripped her off.

He was back on the intravenous drugs, and he was doing them with his ex-wife. I saw him several times with a load of antique furniture and things loaded in the back of his truck, driving around the city. I believe he was spiraling due to his diagnosis. When I went to deliver the divorce papers for his signature, his ex-wife answered the door to the home that we had been living in together. I assumed she was living with him.

The house was extremely dark, and by the time he realized who it was, I was already in my car and driving away. Our divorce was granted a couple of weeks later, and I was once again a free woman. Those first few months after the divorce were difficult. Losing the "love of my life," my "Soulmate," was devastating. I had no real explanation. I was told he did not love me, but he gave me no reason why.

I was just told I had to be gone in ten days, and I argued for thirty. I had divorced, changed jobs, and the bankruptcy was charged off, so I moved on.

Another new beginning – another rebirth – I got my first tattoo at forty-six years old: a butterfly – a tramp stamp, of course!!

Chapter 8: Journey Through the Shadows

I believe the Divine intervened to protect me from contracting HIV, thereby saving my life. In hindsight, it's clear that the Divine was looking out for me, even when I didn't realize it. Despite my anger and resentment—complaining and cursing the Divine for seemingly ruining my life by taking away the one thing I loved after all my repentance, prayers, church attendance, Bible study, communion, and worship—I felt betrayed. Yet, I turned my back on the Divine, but I was never truly alone. The Divine remained by my side, always protecting and guiding my path. Whenever I was in need or felt fear, unsure of how to pay a bill or stretch funds for the month, I reached out to the Divine, who invariably provided solutions. I once thought these ideas were solely mine, but in reality, they were messages from my Higher Self, inspired by the Divine.

This period marked my next Dark Night of the Soul, with depression becoming undeniable. I had been trying to lose weight in the months leading up to this. My daughter and I had a fallout while planning her wedding, which had taken place just a few months before my ex-husband's announcement of divorce. That argument drove me back to smoking, a habit I had quit during our marriage. As many know, divorce can lead to significant weight loss, so I went from a size sixteen to a size four in about five months, and I loved the attention it brought me.

I was attracting men, and my dating profile was getting numerous hits; however, I was merely going through the motions without truly overcoming my depression. Like in the past, I managed to keep it at bay, visiting it occasionally but increasingly dissociating, yet still functioning at a high level. I never missed a day of work, embodying dependability and reliability, accumulating sick days and vacation time I never used. Any unused days were either forfeited under "use it or lose it" policies or compensated for in a minimal payout at the year's end, along with a Christmas bonus. In retrospect, dedicating my life to work resulted in nothing more than old age and loneliness, with little else to show for my efforts.

My daughter encountered some legal troubles, resulting in the loss of custody of my eldest grandson to his father, while my granddaughter was placed in state custody. At that time, my daughter had been in jail for a month, opting to detox rather than have me spend money on a bondsman or attorney. She accepted a plea deal to be released in time for her daughter's fourth birthday. On the day of her release hearing, I unexpectedly encountered both my ex-husband and his ex-wife at the courthouse.

He approached me to express his regrets, confessing he missed me, still loved me, and acknowledged his mistake, expressing a desire to reconcile. I responded that it was too little, too late, advising him to enjoy his time with his ex-wife and requesting that he never contact me again. As I ventured back into the dating scene, I noticed much had changed, and over six years had passed since I was last single, now in my early to mid-40s, navigating the loneliness of nights and weekends without company.

Leaving the church, I was reacquainting myself with solitude, realizing how much of myself I had lost in being what someone else needed. I've come to recognize that I've never truly known who I am, constantly morphing to meet the needs of the moment and the man—be they emotional, mental, physical, or spiritual. This adaptability, a trait groomed into me, ties into my co-dependency and empathetic nature (which I consider a spiritual gift). I have the ability to read a room, sensing sadness, anxiety, fear, and discomfort. While I sometimes view this perceptiveness as a gift, it can also be a curse.

Occasionally, my insight into people's true selves makes them uncomfortable, leading to an immediate dislike for me. This reaction stems from their unease with being seen so clearly.

I joined a dating site and found myself overwhelmed by the sheer number of profiles. There were so many! I spent hours browsing, messaging, texting, talking, and meeting, meeting, meeting! Some prospects were just terrible from the start, not even making it past the messaging phase. I grew so weary of the generic "Hello beautiful!" that unless his profile was particularly appealing, I wouldn't even respond. Then came the slightly varied but still unoriginal compliments like "You're gorgeous," "You're pretty," and "You're so cute." I found myself wishing for something more original. Eventually, if a man's profile photo didn't catch my eye, I wouldn't bother checking his stats.

The ones who made it past the initial phases—the ones I actually met—were hit or miss. Like my mother, after my father left, my luck with men was lacking. There's a saying that "your picker's off," and I suppose that applied to me. My mother encountered a few alcoholics, one overly persistent admirer who sent cards for months—which she found unbearable—and then there was Sully, a married man she might have loved, though not as much as she did my father. When their affair ended, her heart broke, and she never dated again. She worked until retirement and then moved southeast with my little sister. Reflecting on my romantic decisions post-divorce, I noticed a shift in myself, as I ended up dating more married or separated men than single ones. This pattern might be traced back to my father, who had affairs in every country he visited while in the service and in every city we lived in stateside. Perhaps my actions were influenced by an obsession similar to my mother's with my father, an attempt by my Higher Self to understand her perspective. There was a lesson in there, a reason why my mother's life so closely mirrors my own.

It's the generational trauma endured by the women in my family line—adultery, sexual, physical, mental, and spiritual abuse, co-dependency, and persecution for religious beliefs as pagans, witches, and healers. The karma of all the women I have been in my lifetimes has culminated in this one, and through my healing process, I've completed the Karmic Cycle for all of them. We have all healed through my journey.

The next time I saw my ex-husband was at his mother's funeral, a year or more later. They had brought him from prison to pay his last respects. I was there primarily to support my two nieces, who we had in common. After all, it was their grandmother's funeral—she had been both my older sister's and my former mother-in-law's. A part of me also wanted to pay my respects to her, and despite everything, I still cared about him, whether I wanted to admit it to anyone or not.

It wasn't strange or unusual to see him in a denim shirt, dark blue pants, and slip-on canvas rubber-soled shoes, handcuffed with two officers escorting him, one standing on each side. I stepped as close as allowed and told him how sorry I was that she was gone. I got no response. He didn't even look at me. Really? After everything? I tried to show compassion and empathy, and this was the disrespect I received in return.

"Fuck you, asshole!" I thought to myself.

Then, his daughter accused me of sending him love letters in prison. I didn't even know he was in prison, let alone where he was locked up. This was the type of childish, immature behavior I had dealt with from his daughter, mother, and ex-wife when I was his wife. Lies, constant threats of bodily harm, and never any support for me. I was so glad to be rid of all that mess.

My daughter moved in with me for a couple of months after she got out of jail while she was taking classes and preparing to regain custody of her daughter from the state. My friend rented her a room, providing her with a place of residence to help her regain custody of my granddaughter before spring. During that time, she was overcoming a methamphetamine addiction cold turkey outside of rehab. As a result, we spent a lot of time going out to clubs and partying together until she began a new relationship. She started drinking alcohol to replace the high she missed from drugs, a fact I was oblivious to at the time. She was passing her drug tests, so I wasn't concerned about the drinking.

Little did I know it would lead to an alcohol addiction.

My daughter had an affair with an old school buddy (she was always associated with men she knew from school or the neighborhood; all of her pals had slept together, every lady had sex with every guy, and they were all related by DNA).To my knowledge, she has only "dated" two men who weren't in her buddy group or from our area. My youngest grandchild was born to her; a few months after he was born, they were married. Up until the infant was two, they were content. Since he was young, her husband had a severe anxiety illness, and he started looking for medication other than what was prescribed to him. After he lost his job, things became worse.

We were still going out once in a while when she was married, but I did not like going out alone. So, I spent years reviewing profiles, even if most of the men I encountered were "red flag Rogers." If they made it through the entire process, they would make it halfway through the meal, and boom! A red flag! I would finally find someone half decent; you know you can't have it all; you have to take the good with the bad. We would date for a couple of months, and then I would get ghosted, or he would do something completely suspicious, and I would have to cut him loose. This went on for a couple of years.

I met this one guy from the site. He was handsome, lived nearby, had a great job, was really interested in me, and was completely and totally single (no legal attachments); the only thing that made me hesitant was he had a small child that lived with him, a son. I did not like having to deal with baby mamas, and that was a big red flag! But I thought I would see how it went since you have to take the good with the bad sometimes.

My apartment complex was raising the rent by about fifty dollars a month, and I was not making enough money to pay that much rent. I was panicking because I needed a place in thirty days. His mobile home park had a home available for rent. I should have known it was a bad idea, but the rent was the right price, and I really needed a place on short notice, so I moved in.

It was almost immediately that things changed. Things were good between us, except he had a bedroom problem. He could not get it up, and if he did get it up, he couldn't keep it up. His last relationship was extremely abusive emotionally and mentally. He never went into detail. But I believe it had to do with S&M, and he couldn't perform without it and was ashamed to ask for it. I can't say for sure, but it's what my intuition is telling me, and I'm usually right.

Something was strange because his baby mama lived in another city several miles away, and it didn't seem like she was interested in seeing her son on a regular basis. He kept telling me it wasn't my fault. I don't know; he started dating someone else because I saw her a couple of times before he moved out. As usual, I would fall for these guys, and they would ghost me.

I decided it was time to take a break, maybe just concentrate on work and myself, not worry about dating so much. I had moved into this new place only one month prior and was just starting to settle in. So, I put my home together. I hung what I could on the walls (it's hard to hang things in a mobile home) and really made it mine. Things were normal, and I moved at my normal pace. My moods fluctuated as they normally did, but now, they seem to do that a bit more often.

I have experienced mood swings since I was about thirteen or fourteen years old (I wonder why). I knew others' lives were different from mine. I knew that because others were laughing and joyful. They had friends and boyfriends, they were popular, pretty, wore nice clothes, all the things I wasn't. Everyone liked them; they were the cheerleaders and prom queens. I knew there was something different about me. Not only the obvious things, my looks, my trauma, and my home life, but something else. Something I couldn't explain, but I knew it was there. I had felt it since I was a young child. I was special somehow. I was meant to be someone. I could feel it.

From the first time I felt it, I knew that I needed counseling/therapy – psychiatric care. I never could afford it, even with insurance. The deductible was outrageous, and once that was met, you still had to pay $175.00 an hour out of your own pocket as a co-pay amount. I needed to go at least three times a week, so that was out of the question. The only solution I had was to dissociate any type of hurt or trauma that I experienced on a day-to-day basis.

No matter how small, just push it down – ignore it – dissociate from it. I had become an expert at this after all; at that time, I had been doing it for thirty-three years. I didn't know that was what I was doing, but I realize now that it is what saved my life emotionally, physically, mentally, and spiritually. This protected my mental state. It kept me sane. It kept me functioning, able to maintain a normal life (as normal-looking and functioning as possible to the outside world) like everyone else. Work, home, kids, church – day in and day out – just like everyone else.

Ignore your feelings – stuff the anger – don't cry, that shows weakness – if you don't ask for help, that makes you a strong woman – it makes you an independent woman – I don't need anyone, I can do it all on my own – you can't trust anyone but yourself – you can't count on anyone but yourself. These are the things I used to tell myself because this is the only way I knew how to survive. This created anxiety, stress, and depression – just writing this gives me chest palpitations. By this time, I had spent close to twenty-one years basically estranged from my family. My normal weekday schedule became working your average eight-hour day, and my nights and weekends were spent feeding cats, cleaning litterboxes, doing household chores, weekly laundry, and occasionally shopping (this was before pickup or delivery).

I spent money on useless items that I thought I needed, but I really didn't; I could live without them. I had given up searching for my "Soulmate" or my next relationship and was just existing. Fighting depression, something that was a daily thing, I had just become so used to feeling that way it had just become who I was, a part of my personality. So, I only noticed the depression when it got extremely bad and out of control. It was slowly creeping in – a little darker each day. It can creep in so slowly that you don't even notice until it takes you over.

I was becoming extremely unhappy in my profession; my love life was non-existent; I was meeting men, but there was something wrong with every one of them; I had no friends to go and do things with. I hate going places alone; you have no one to talk to about what you are doing, and eating alone really sucks!

I dated a couple of men during the next year and a half, but only a couple of months apiece. I was just getting tired of the clubs and the whole driving all the drunks to and from the bar, mainly my daughter and her friends. They would drink while getting ready and be drunk by the time we left to go to the club, and by the time we got to the club, they were drinking all night until closing, and then I would have to find them, gather them all up like children, and pile them all in the car.

They would want to go to breakfast and act ridiculous in public. I was the only sober one out of all of them. It was always a hassle, and I just got tired of it. They were belligerent, rude, and embarrassing. They would treat me shitty, and they would not remember it the next day, so I quit going.

I was beginning to slide deeper into the depression that I had been in my entire life; at the time, I didn't know it was just the beginning of a long winter in my Soul. Being unhappy with my life is putting it mildly. This is the true start of my Dark Night of the Soul. This lasted a total of approximately seventeen years because I didn't or wouldn't heed the warning signs. My Higher Self had been calling me since I was eighteen after my rape, but I was too young to understand. This time, I was old enough to hear, understand, and heed it. I knew I needed help – I just wasn't getting it.

My depression – my real and most excruciating Dark Night of the Soul was beginning, and it was going to get much darker before the light came in. The continuation of the original Dark Night of the Soul – it had just been getting darker and darker every time I had a heartbreak, a financial block, the loss of a job, or some sort of calamity, but I didn't recognize it, because I had no idea what it was. I just kept pushing it down and dissociating. I just kept ignoring it, thinking it would just go away.

The women in my family have always been high-strung, loud, and what I consider hateful, spiteful, and petty. I believe we are all neurodivergent with bipolar tendencies but have been diagnosed as bipolar, but none of them want to be diagnosed with either, admit they are either, or want to get any kind of treatment for either. My daughter was the one to discover the "bi-polar" genetic trait in our family tree. My granddaughter, who was seven years old at the time, was having a lot of trouble controlling herself when it came to her anger and impulses. She was having outbursts, and she would hurt her little brother and act out at school. She had kicked a teacher in one incident, even though, from her side of the story, it was in self-defense. She took up for a little girl when a bully was picking on her, but she got physical with the bully and was suspended from school for three days. She was taken to a psychiatrist and a medical doctor located in the same office so they could consult regarding her medication and treatment since they specialized in young children and adolescents.

They diagnosed her with bipolar disorder and informed my daughter about the diagnosis, disorder, symptoms, and how it can be inherited genetically. She was placed on medication for a year and then weaned off of them. My daughter was discussing it with me and recognized some character traits similar to my emotional outbursts when I would get upset or triggered and my outbursts of anger at the littlest things, my OCD, and other symptoms. She encouraged me to seek a consultation, which led me to my diagnosis.

However, I have been on medication for over ten years, and I wish I had never started taking it. I have to say, I feel less cognitive, and I worry about the medications I have taken as they all can result in memory loss, and my father died from Alzheimer's. I have also seen an article regarding women being neurodivergent and being incorrectly diagnosed as bipolar. I'm researching this for myself just for a second opinion option. It's also interesting how my daughter berates me for "skills, not pills" to heal my bipolar disorder, but it was her idea in the first place to get diagnosed and medication. I have cut down the dosage myself, trying to get off the medication cold turkey, and am manifesting mental clarity, mental health, and cognitive and memory healing. I am no physician and do not recommend anyone doing this yourself – do as your physician recommends, but, myself, I am turning to holistic and as natural as possible treatments as I can get and use.

Also, please note you need to do some sort of therapy, counseling, or psychiatric therapy with medication or without medication, depending on your circumstances. Any type of abuse, whether it be physical, emotional, sexual, mental, or even spiritual, requires professional counseling or therapy of some form or fashion, whether you are prescribed medication or not.

I have not had any counseling on my Spiritual Awakening Journey, and this has made my journey a bit more challenging for me. Releasing the emotional trauma and forgiving myself, as well as others, has taken many years longer than it should have. I have used meditation and talk therapy. My talk therapy is speaking aloud to the Divine. I have recorded my conversations on my phone and noticed that as I spoke, profound statements and ideas came to my mind.

I had conversations with the Divine – I talked about my journey, how I was struggling, or how I was feeling about my energy that day – I even yelled, cussed at, and cried with the Divine, and that is when I got the most profound answers. I got responses to the questions I asked. I got confirmation by seeing Cardinals or crows fly by the window or butterflies out of season.

The Divine and my Higher Self took me inward, and I touched and held the hands of my Inner Child. I danced with her, twirled in circles, cried with joy, laughed aloud, and gave her the emotional healing she had needed for so long. Making up for all the emotional neglect, I spend time with her through meditation, healing, and strengthening my relationship with my Higher Self, Christ's consciousness, and the Divine, increasing my power and my divination.

My daughter and her husband's relationship began to become rockier not long after this time due to his addiction to valium and anti-anxiety drugs. About that time, an old boyfriend (the one that she received her felony child neglect charges and drug charges over) had gotten out of prison, and she just could not stay away from him. So, what do you think happened? She began an affair with him and left her husband. She had no job and no place to stay.

She showed up on my doorstep with my two young grandchildren because I had two extra rooms and an extra bathroom, with the convict in tow. I could not say no to her without saying no to my grandchildren; I couldn't take them in without her because I had to work and couldn't stay home and watch the baby. She knew she had me right where she wanted me – and as usual – every damn time, I would have to let her in.

I always cleaned up after her, ensuring she was taken care of and her needs met – oh! But to hear her tell it, she had done it all on her own, and I was a horrible mother – I was abusive – never did anything for her – she never had anyone's help – she has always done it on her own. Even my children talked to me like I was unworthy of love and appreciation.

As though I didn't deserve respect or validation for the times I had rescued her - from jail, paid electric, water, and gas bills, bought parts for her car, paid months of rent, car insurance, and phone bills, and given her my medical insurance proceeds for my injuries from my car accident; there is so much more. But these things are forgotten when resentment is the only emotion you allow yourself to experience from your pain.

The living arrangements were never kosher, to say the least. Her boyfriend's constant jealousy led to constant fighting; she would drink; they would fight – it would get physical – I would call the cops; I would tell the truth about what was going on; she would say, "We have been drinking, I fell, or I ran into the door...." She would not press charges; the cops would leave, and five minutes later, they were beating each other.

This went on for at least two years, if not three.

She ended up with a busted nose, numerous black eyes, broken foot/ankle, broken wrist/hand/fingers; he split her scalp open down to the bone, and she wouldn't go for stitches because there would be questions; he choked her to unconsciousness (to death twice) several times – this man tried to kill her more than once. The police officers were called so many times because of them fighting in the front yard and street at 3:00 a.m., in the morning, that the landlord evicted me. I had never had an eviction in my life.

I lost my job during this abusive and hectic invasion of my home due to my attitude and depressive state. I was miserable, and my employer could see it. The four years of service didn't matter to them. I was depressed and miserable; it showed on my face. It was bad for everyone else's morale, and they wanted me out of there. I had passed out in the bathroom from one of my medications, and it was only a couple of weeks before I was let go with six weeks' worth of severance pay.

That started my spiraling. Things were spinning out of my control!

This added to the Dark Night of the Soul that had been slowly building over the years, starting back when I should have started my Spiritual Awakening Journey - going inward to find my Inner Child in order to heal my trauma, which would have connected me with my Higher Self, which would have brought me closer to the Divine, in order to find that self-love and acceptance that we all search for in others that you can find in yourself and in the Divine.

By August 2013, I was working for an insurance company as a temporary employee, hoping the job would become permanent. I was checking in on the dating site occasionally when my phone would show a notice of a message. I had gained some weight and was not really expecting anyone to be hitting my profile when this guy sent me a message.

I had sworn off "separated" men because I had been burned so many times, but for some reason, I just thought, give this guy a chance; I thought a year of separation was a safe time. I responded, and we set up a meeting to have coffee at the local coffee shop.

Chapter 9: Unexpected Reconnections

He arrived on his motorcycle. He was not as good-looking as in the photograph he had posted, but I was a little heavier than in my last photo, so I figured each of us was just staying to be polite. He had never been there before, so I ordered my usual for us both, and we sat down outside. We sat there until the shop closed, and neither of us wanted the conversation to end. We headed to I Hop for more coffee. It was the best time I had had in quite a long time.

The conversation just flowed so easily; we liked the same things – disliked the same things, and laughed at each other's jokes. We enjoyed the same music and movies; this was too good to be true. He was younger, but only by a couple of years, which was no big deal. This was amazing! It was getting late (way past midnight), and he had to work the next day, so I took him back to his bike. He hugged me goodbye and left me, hoping I would see him again.

He texted me a bit later to let me know he had made it home safely. We spoke a couple of days later and set up a movie date for that coming weekend. He called on Wednesday to tell me he could not see me again. He was really upset when I asked why, and he started to cry because he had lied to me. He had not been separated for a year; he had only been separated for two months. He was extremely upset because he did not like lying to people. I calmed him down, forgave him for lying, and reassured him (against my better judgment – but I was really drawn to this man) that I would continue seeing him. This should have been my first red flag. But I felt a strong connection to this man.

A couple of weeks after we met, my birthday came around. He asked me what my favorite cake was, and I let him know it was German Chocolate. If I remember correctly, it was his mother's favorite as well. He took it upon himself to make a birthday cake for me from SCRATCH!!

It was beautifully done and tasted great!! I was so impressed and touched by the sentimental and, for lack of a better word, loving gesture. I had never known such attention.

Sweet voicemails when I couldn't get to the phone (me panicking because I missed his call – old patterns are hard to break); being pleased first before he took pleasure; cooking together; following through with doing what he said he was going to do, and if he was unable to do so, there was a call or text in plenty of time for me to alternate my plans. He was just as excited to see me as I was to see him. He was always there, always on time, on Fridays to pick me up for the weekend. I was not used to being treated well. I believe this is why I fell for him, hard and so fast. I absolutely love bombing!!

For the first time since my last husband (the man I had been crazy about since childhood), I felt a pull that was almost uncomfortable; of course, this was a co-dependency thing; I was going to show him the love he wasn't getting from the wife that left him for another man, once again I was going to play the role she couldn't or wouldn't play—the savior. I had not felt attracted to someone like this in a long time and didn't want to lose it. It was like he had been made for me. He was there in the right place at the right time.

I convinced him (which should have been another red flag) that everything would be fine, and we started seeing each other on a regular basis. I began spending weekends with him at his home, and we talked and texted every day. One Saturday morning, after spending the night at my home with me, he got up to head to a tile job he needed to finish (he had his own small tile company at the time); when he kissed me goodbye, and then he said, "I love you."

I was shocked (ecstatic to hear him say it) and not sure what to say. It had been almost three months, and things were great between us. I had met his family and spent Thanksgiving with them; they seemed to like me. I loved him too and had been waiting for him to say it first, and here it was – "I love you too" came out of my mouth almost instantly.

I am not sure when or how the communication started, but his wife suddenly needed someone to take care of the two dogs she had taken with her when she left him for her drug-dealing lover. While they had been together, my boyfriend had been out of town driving a truck, sending money home - she hadn't been paying the mortgage and bills; had spent all the money he was sent home on drugs and this other man, and when my boyfriend found out about it, he came home to an empty house and bank account. Obviously, she and her lover had fought and needed somewhere to go in a hurry. We went and picked up the two dogs.

Now, one of the dogs, Scooter, was a dog that my boyfriend owned with her, so he was extremely happy to have his dog back. My intuition knew that my time was growing quickly to a close. Christmas was approaching, and she was coming home because the money and drugs had run out; she knew he still loved her and would take her back, and she had no place to spend the holiday. It was not long before I was dumped, and that was the end of it. I took it harder than I thought I would. I fell hard for him because we just fit so perfectly. We treated each other with respect, consideration, compassion, empathy, and tenderness. We meshed intimately (I had never felt so comfortable and uninhibited with someone before, not even my last husband, and I had been with him for thirteen years, especially after my years of pushing down my uncomfortableness with sex in general and my loss of sexual desire from medication). This guy was deep in my heart, deeper than even I had experienced. I missed him terribly and the intimacy.

The winter of 2013/2014 was cold and dark for me. The house even seemed darker than usual; my bedroom had one window, and my dresser mirror covered it. My bedroom was dark and gloomy, and I spent as little time there as possible. It made me more depressed. My daughter was working on her second year of college, going to school to get her Associate's Degree, which added to the usual trouble with her partner's insecurities and mental illness. She, of course, worked at a local bar as a waitress, which was more fuel for the fire. She was drinking, hanging out, and dancing in the bar on her nights off or drinking at home – more fuel!

I could not escape it – it never ended!! Every day – every night – the same thing!!

Drinking, fighting, police officers – exhausting!! He was diagnosed as schizophrenic and bipolar while they were living with me. Her behavior never changed to accommodate his diagnosis. For the past three months, I had been going on the weekends to escape it, and it had been escalating, and it was getting completely out of control!

Christmas and the New Year were sad. My ex-boyfriend's birthday was December 31st, and it was one of the worst New Year's I had experienced. I had spent a lot of them alone over the last seven years. I was such a sucker for punishment I sent him text messages on Christmas and his birthday but never received a response. I pushed it as far out of my mind as I could, but it was not easy. No one had ever treated me so well. The attention I received from him was mesmerizing, and I craved it. The more he ignored me, the worse it got.

The depression that I had fallen into and my attitude because of the first two years of living with the abusive relationship between my daughter and her partner was overwhelming. I was on medication, but it was not enough to change my outlook fast enough. Whether people know it or not, abusive relationships affect the entire family. Living in flight or fight mode constantly— the stress and anxiety on the body can be physically, mentally, and emotionally damaging.

Living with that every day for weeks, months, YEARS!

The damage we are doing to women, children, and, yes, even men is immense!! I had been living in that mode since I was twelve years old – did not realize it until much later in life when I had been doing it for over forty years – so this living situation was just adding to it. All the medication I was taking was doing absolutely nothing; it was an entire waste of money. So now rocky employment, physically abusive relationship in the house, how to cover expenses when he is the only one bringing in steady money and you cannot even get his share of the rent on a regular basis. You add that on top of all the regular everyday anxiety you have, and you have a recipe for a Dark Night of the Soul.

I have been challenged many times. I have always found a way to provide an escape route for any problem. I need money for a bill, a car part, groceries, and gas money. I cannot think of one time that I haven't been sent or found a way to cover every financial need or necessity I needed in my life. This is one of the many lessons you will begin to learn as you take a look inside yourself, heal your Inner Child, integrate your Inner Child, Higher Self, and Spirit, and step away from the media and all the things in society (which is what people refer to as the "Matrix") that keep your mind busy, and begin to focus on the real purpose for our existence, your Spiritual Awakening Journey. You realize that it is the Divine that has provided those escape routes, not you – that's ego. I did not understand this at the time. Be sure to recognize the Divine and be grateful every day for what is provided to you. The more grateful you are, the more will come to you.

I pushed forward, grew more depressed, and discussed my medication more than I discussed my depression with the psych that was assigned to me that month. It never failed: increase the dosage of this medication, decrease this dosage in this medication, and add two more; one was an anti-depressant for my anti-depressant. By now, I have been on medication for about four years. I was not getting counseling of any kind, and the medication basically stopped working. I was just walking around in a zombie-like state. I did not feel anything, not happy – not sad, just nothing. The chemicals were supposed to balance the serotonin and dopamine in the brain. If balancing those two chemicals in the brain makes you feel no emotions, no thank you. I no longer wanted to feel this way. This has gone on for fourteen years, so I am trying to make changes. I recently got into my car and could not remember where I was going. It took a couple of minutes for me to remember where I was headed.

This frightened me. I've had moments driving where I couldn't remember where I was supposed to be going. Times where I did not recognize where I was. Signs and symptoms of dementia. Something must be done now.

The temporary job at the insurance company had run its course, and in February 2014, I found a full-time job—one of the worst jobs I have ever had. I remember feeling utterly miserable. I loathed my living situation and my job. I was nursing a broken heart, refereeing fights in the middle of the night while trying to get enough rest to work all day the next. I struggled to pay the bills, and my depression cast a dark shadow over me, following me around like the Grim Reaper. This period only deepened the Dark Night of the Soul.

My Dark Night of the Soul probably initially began the first time my father took me into that bathroom. With each traumatic experience and each difficult situation I faced alone (which was constant), I was thrown deeper into depression and further into darkness. These experiences brought me closer to my Spiritual Awakening Journey to heal my Inner Child, even as she continued to suffer. Little did I know it would take forty-six years to actually begin the journey.

It was near the end of April or the beginning of May 2014 when I received a text from the man over whom I had been grieving. I was shocked and excited simultaneously. It turned out his wife had once again left him for her lover, and this time, she wanted a divorce. During their time together, she had spent a great deal of time asking questions about me. Foolishly, he answered them. I can't fathom why he would do something so reckless. He shared his feelings about me, our intimacy, and personal details. He even drove her by my house once or twice, which made me extremely uncomfortable and angry. But it was too late; there was nothing I could do about it. After she left (a couple of weeks before he contacted me), he drove by himself several times. He wanted to call and text but was afraid I wouldn't respond.

But I was prepared to rescue this man once again, being the glutton for punishment that I am, craving love so badly, and being the people-pleasing, co-dependent person I am. I was going to love him into happiness and make him truly love me by being everything he needed me to be. While I was at it, I was going to be loved the way I have always wanted and deserved to be. He had chosen me after all!! Here we go again!

Now that she had left him for the second time, he seemed angrier with her and a bit more determined to have a relationship with me, but I read the situation completely wrong. I was so convinced that this man felt the same way about me that I did not see that was not the case. I thought, once again, that I had found my actual Soulmate, not realizing that my Soulmate would never be connected to someone else. Divine timing surely would require both of you to be without any binding to others. During this time, my daughter, her abusive partner, and my grandchildren were still residing with me, and I was still spending every weekend with my man, not knowing that all hell was breaking loose on the weekends.

I received an eviction notice because of all the police activity occurring at my home while I was gone on the weekends during the few weeks since I had rekindled my relationship. Her boyfriend had been banned from the house, but she was sneaking him in at night while I was sleeping. She never respected me or the rules in my house. She always just took over my homes, made her own rules, and just did as she pleased. My stress and anxiety were through the roof. I had just started a new job and couldn't ask for time off to go to court for an eviction hearing; I had to find a place to stay with an eviction on my record, come up with close to $3,000 to move with a deposit, rent, utility fees, etc., and no place to go.

As the Divine always does, he provided a way out. My boyfriend came out of nowhere to be my hero. He offered to let me move in with him, and I jumped at the chance. My daughter did not like the idea because I guess she thought I would move out with her, her partner, and my grandchildren and live in the hell that I had been stuck in for the last three years. Sorely mistaken!!! I moved in with him and left her my entire household – my washer and dryer, my furniture, and the full kitchen (dishes, pots and pans, utensils).

All I took was my personal stuff, my collectible stuff, knickknacks, personal furniture, and my cat. In fact, I rented a huge U-Haul truck (paid for it myself), and my boyfriend moved my stuff and my daughter's stuff – all by himself to homes and storage units- all in one day. But she was still angry that I was not moving with them and abandoning her and her children. Living with him was absolute bliss for me. Despite disliking the drive from the town where his house was to downtown, where I worked, the time spent with him during my downtime made it all worthwhile. I can't recall the exact reason, but while we were living together, he began working for a tow truck company. I would accompany him on calls during weekends and holidays just to spend time together, as he was on call 24 hours a day, typically seven days a week, with only one day or weekend off every six weeks or so. To spend some time with him, I essentially had to go along on these trips. Those journeys are among my favorite memories.

I also cherish the memory of riding on the back of his Harley along a back road on a hot summer evening at dusk. The road was shaded by trees lining the south side, creating a cool breeze even though the temperature was in the 100s. I felt free—no worries, just happiness and love.

However, this bliss was short-lived; things soon began to change. He took me to buy my birthday gifts—a pair of Harley boots and a pink crystal skull ring. Shortly after, he stopped coming to bed after returning from two calls, even when it was early, before 1:00 a.m. It took me about two weeks to notice. I observed him becoming distant and not as tender or sweet as before. He seemed colder and more aloof. There was a palpable shift; I could sense a change in his energy. My intuition was fully alert. I confronted the issue, asking him what was wrong, noting that something had changed, and expressing my need to understand. His eyes filled with tears, and he struggled to speak.

This difficulty suggested to me that he must have had feelings for me; otherwise, it wouldn't have been so hard for him to say the words. He told me he needed me to move out by October 1st.

This conversation took place in the middle of September, and I argued that it was impossible for me to find an apartment in two weeks, let alone gather all the necessary funds. I requested that you secure a place until the first of November. He seemed to understand, but she didn't. He had been talking to her for a few weeks, which explained the guilt and shame behind the birthday gifts—it was his way of compensating for "cheating" on me with her.

He had begun smoking synthetic marijuana, which caused him to pass out immediately. Watching it happen frightened me. I attempted to discuss the issue with him. He confessed that he loved me and believed I was the better woman for him, yet he still harbored feelings for her and wanted to be with her. We navigated through this challenging period for a month, eventually ending the relationship on good terms. We never engaged in arguments, harsh words, or name-calling. There was only one thing I said that I have ever regretted: wishing that his wife would die from either a drug overdose or a seizure, which had begun due to her drug addiction.

Throughout October, he was under immense pressure, juggling her jealousy over me and our living situation while also dealing with my heartbreak as he watched me cry and mope around. He assured her that he would not sleep with me or have any physical contact with me—no kissing, nothing. We simply coexisted in the same house until I could leave.

However, his feelings for me were too strong to ignore completely. There were moments of weakness, times when he desired me, and we became intimate. His feelings for me remained unchanged, although the intimacy felt somewhat different, possibly because he started feeling guilty each time it happened, but the emotion was still present.

During this time, I had gone into town to get my nails done. While driving north on a major street in my SUV, a small car headed south on the same road crossed my path. There were no stop signs or traffic lights in the area we were in. I had the right of way, but she decided to make a left-hand turn across two lanes.

Traveling at 45 mph in a 45 mph zone, I attempted to stop, but there wasn't enough time – I broadsided her! The collision sent both of us spinning – I ended up facing southbound, and she ended up northbound. It was a severe accident. I assume bystanders called 911 because, before I knew it, someone was unbuckling my seat belt. Next, a fireman was beside me, instructing me not to move while I insisted I needed to get out and check on my car. Despite my protests that I was fine, they placed me in a neck brace, secured me to a backboard, and loaded me into an ambulance.

Across from me in the ambulance was the woman responsible for the accident. She kept apologizing, but I didn't say a word. I was so furious that I didn't dare speak; it was best just to keep quiet. The police officer's attitude when he arrived was appalling; he was nearly yelling at her, bombarding her with questions about alcohol, medication, drugs, and her whereabouts before and after the accident.

When it was time to leave for the hospital, the ambulance driver intended to take us to the ambulance service's affiliated hospital. However, the other driver protested, insisting on being taken to a hospital of her choice. It seemed further away than the one initially chosen, and the ambulance crew appeared irritated at having to go out of their way, but ultimately, she was taken to her preferred hospital.

Chapter 10: Cycle of Heartbreak

"Blessed are the poor in spirit, for theirs is the kingdom of heaven. Blessed are those who mourn, for they will be comforted. Blessed are the meek, for they will inherit the earth. Blessed are those who hunger and thirst for righteousness, for they will be filled. Blessed are the merciful, for they will be shown mercy. Blessed are the pure in heart, for they will see God. Blessed are the peacemakers, for they will be called children of God. Blessed are those who are persecuted because of righteousness, for theirs is the kingdom of heaven."
—Mathew Chapter 5, Verse 2-10

I was covered in Starbucks Venti Mocha Frappuccino (a brand new one I had just purchased, along with a full tank of gas before the accident). I was beginning to get sore, but I was still in shock and still pumped with adrenaline, so I was just getting frustrated. They had me standing up against the wall on a bodyboard in the room so they could take an x-ray of my back. I'm laying there in my wet pants, shaking because they keep it so cold in hospitals. I just wanted to go home and start figuring out how the hell I was going to get to work come Monday morning until I could get a new car. This could possibly set me back on moving out; who knew?

I called him to get a ride home from the hospital, and he thought I was lying about the accident and being at the hospital because she had lied in the past to get him to do things for her and manipulate him. I was so mad when he showed up, and I proved him wrong. He apologized, but I was so angry and hurt that he would compare me to her. I was so much better than her; how dare he?

Even though he was avoiding me as much as possible, one night, when he was wasted on his fake weed right after he had gotten in from a call, we were engaged in intercourse, and a vehicle had pulled into the driveway. The next thing we knew, someone was beating on the front door. He threw on his pants as quickly as he could and went to the front door. It was his wife; she was beating on the door, and when he answered it, she was trying to push her way into the house. She knew he had been in my bed, and she wanted a piece of me because of it.

She had finally pushed past him and was headed for the bedroom door. He caught her in time, and when she discovered she could not get past him, she headed through the kitchen to the back door that led through the bathroom into the master bedroom. It was already locked, and she couldn't get in. When she realized he was protecting me at all costs and that she could not get to me, she was even more angry; she was hysterical - yelling, cussing, and she really wanted to kick my ass. I cannot remember how he got her to leave.

I recall that when she was outside, she was throwing things at the bedroom window where the bed was sitting, and I was still in the bedroom, sitting on the chair in the corner next to the windows. He kept telling her to stop, and the window never broke. I overheard him telling her that the glass was shatterproof and that she was wasting her time. Eventually, she left, but not after she made it very clear she wanted me gone.

I found an apartment at the old apartment complex where I had an apartment when I left my ex-husband back in 2006. Right back where I started (this should have been a sign – a wake-up call). The time came to pack up what little I had unpacked to live there – clothes, bathroom items, nothing more than that. I had left my entire household behind because he had everything (what little we needed) to set up a home. He could not move me out fast enough.

She kept calling all day – "Is she out yet – I thought she would be out by noon." It's no wonder it took us all day to move it. It was just him and I loading, driving 20 miles from the house in the country to the apartment in the city – unloading – repeat. We did two loads this way.

I did not have much to move, of course; I had no household items. I had to start all over again. I took the brand-new television that we had purchased and the sectional that he had bought from Goodwill after she had left and took all his furniture. It was too big for the apartment, but I needed some furniture, and it was the least he could do, leaving me high and dry since I had no household items.

Once again, I was devastated and facing starting all over again from scratch. He told me he would keep in touch, that he still loved me, and that he would miss me too. He said all of that to appease me so he could get the hell out of there so he could get across town and pick her up because she was on his ass for spending more time with me than necessary.

I spent the rest of that weekend putting the place together and facing the prospect that I might end up alone for the rest of my life. The Dark Night of the Soul got darker, and this is where it got the darkest it ever had. That apartment was filled with dark shadows. The bedroom, no matter how bright the lightbulbs I put in the ceiling fan - that room was always dark – pitch black without the lights on. Open the shades, and it would have a bit of light, but it is generally always shadowed. There were no trees; it was on the south side of the building. There were no obstructions to block the top of the window; still, it was dark. The apartment was set up to have southern light come in from the large living and dining room windows, but the porch had a cover over it, so the sun was blocked in the living room, and the dining room window was covered with the upstairs apartment's staircase, so it was always dark. It fit my mood, though, and maybe my mood turned the apartment into a dungeon.

I hated this place; it was cold and impersonal. I did not hang anything on the walls because I hadn't planned on being there forever, but I was there for almost seven years. My cat was the only thing that had been constant in my life since 2006. He helped me through my depression by just being there. He did not have to be on my lap; I didn't have to be petting him; just him being in the house was enough to keep me from feeling as lonely as I could have felt. I know that sounds crazy, but it is true.

Of course, being a cat, he was on my lap as much as he could be; he slept on me in my bed at night. He watched me shower, get ready, and dress for work in the mornings. He was and will always be my best friend, even though I lost him in November 2023.

I struggled to get over the love that I had lost, so I just ignored my feelings, the pain, and the depression. I focused on my job (which I just hated; it was the worst!! – I wanted to quit!!) and tried to find something to keep my mind busy. I had my weaker moments and sent texts and voice messages. No responses from him, of course, but I did receive a letter from her.

As usual, he had given her my address, and he probably drove her by my apartment, for that matter. She, of course, called me names, put me down, called me old, told me his family did not like me, that he had spoken badly about me - you name it, she said it. She threatened me and told me to stay away from her husband, the usual stuff, high school stuff. I put the letter away for safekeeping, but I do not know why; I just did. I just ran across it this year in a bunch of papers I have not looked at in six years; I threw it away. Letting go of and throwing away things that do not serve my highest good – letting go of all the old emotional trauma – everything is holding me back. I suppose finally letting go of him, and her, for that matter.

Thanksgiving, Christmas, and New Year came and went, but nothing spectacular happened. I had spent so much time alone during the past eight holiday seasons that it seemed just like extra days off from the hellhole I worked in, just a couple of extra days to stay up late, watch some television, smoke some good grass, and sleep in. I didn't decorate for the holidays; I hadn't done so in 8 years, so there's no reason to start now. I would go over to my daughter's home on Christmas Eve to get the traditional pj's; we would drink hot cocoa, eat popcorn, and watch a movie. I would open my gift (always a fucking coffee cup – never any thought or love put into the gift – pj's always too big).

During the three Christmas days I spent with them, during the three years they lived with me, I got a stocking from her, but I did not before then. I spent a great deal of money on them for Christmas. I took the time to figure out what they wanted or needed. I made sure that it was something they would – you would think to be grateful for – but I would get nothing (not a gift), not even a thank you. They would look at it and set it aside, never saying a word. Like it was expected, no big deal. I purchased a virtual game program with the headset and all the required components during the final Christmas I spent with my youngest grandchildren. They used it twice, and there was no excitement, nothing. Now, I know they knew it was coming, but you would think there would be some sort of reaction.

It has been that way since they were small. They have no reaction to anything you do for them, no matter what it is. No appreciation, no thank you; it is like it's expected as you owe it to them. My daughter was the same way towards me. It was like she expected me to do things for her to make up for the abuse and neglect she suffered as a child, things I had already validated her and her feelings for, acknowledged, owned, and apologized for. She never forgave me, and there is nothing further I can do on my part.

I am working on this journey; I have been released of all that does not serve my higher good. I have had to release the old to receive the new. She and my grandchildren chose to walk away from me and block all communications with me. That was not my choice, but I had to complete my Karmic Cycle by having people and things that I loved taken from me, releasing those things that did not serve my higher good, and letting go of those that are no longer vibrating on my frequency, this is why they made that choice, the Divine removed them as they are not a part of the plan. If these people are to be a part of the plan or my journey, they will be brought back into my life in Divine timing. I went to the 2015 Fleetwood Mac concert with a man that I found out later was a narcissist; he was controlling and absolutely crazy. He was an over-the-road truck driver. I would be on the phone with him at lunch from noon to 1:00 p.m. if he wasn't sleeping, and from 5:00 p.m. until I went to bed at 10:00 p.m. every day, Monday through Sunday, and when he was in town, I spent every day with him. There were a few red flags, but I tolerated him because I only had to deal with him every 10 to 15 days in town, and it gave me someone to fill the time at night on the phone.

During the time I had entered and exited my ex-boyfriend's life, my daughter had moved into a home with her partner, and during their last physical altercation, he choked her to death (literally); she had passed out for two minutes. When she came to, she found him in the front yard with the police officers handcuffing him. He had been taken to jail, the state was filing charges, whether she was or not, and he was going to do some prison time for these charges. She had no job, was behind on rent, and needed help. I gave her my insurance proceeds from the accident I had before moving out of my ex-boyfriend's house to pay some back rent and three months' rent in advance.

She started working and began to get things together. I thought she was drinking constantly; she was spiraling without him – she was troubled – emotionally, mentally, physically, and especially spiritually – she has told me she was having a Dark Night of the Soul. He would call her from jail, and she would live for those calls. I am not an expert on the symptoms, causes, etc., of alcoholism, drug addiction, or abusive relationships. I do know that it is hard to walk away from an abuser or a relationship involving those circumstances. She struggled without him just as much as she struggled with him.

I could not understand it, but I sympathized with her. I could see her pain, and I knew how it hurt to love someone you knew was not good for you, but you wanted and needed and loved them anyway. From what she has shared with me, her alcoholism really began at this point. I did not know how dark her life had gotten. I did not know how bad it was for her. She was never one to reach out to me when she needed emotional support, so I never knew her deepest feelings, her darkest moments, or her need for support.

I had told the insurance company that I had worked for a year prior as a temporary employee and that if the temporary position ever became a full-time position, I was absolutely interested and to give me a call. And the manager was so impressed with my performance and work ethic that she reassured me that she would. I had spent all morning on a stack of mail that was at least two feet tall, scanning it in and saving it to the electronic file and then putting it in the box to be shredded; it took all morning. Now I have to get back from lunch (which was spent at the psych clinic for a checkup to get a refill on my medication) and start the stuff that would have been done this morning if the mail hadn't taken so long. I had been having the worst day that day; then, I got "the call" from my old manager from the insurance company.

The position had opened up, and it was now a full-time position; she had chosen me, but I had to go through the regular red tape routine. She wanted me to come into the office to fill out the application on the website; they would set up the interview and get me started. I was so excited. This was just what I had been hoping (and silently praying for).

The guy I had been talking to every day for a couple of months and was aware of the situation with my job and how unhappy I was. I had confided in him about how they had been treating me and how I was overwhelmed with more responsibilities than I was hired to do. I wanted a new job badly. The year on this job I had shown to be a mistake. I had been forced to quit smoking because it cost extra for my insurance premium, and they did not like me taking two 10-minute breaks a day outside in my car. Then, I could not vape in the kitchen and answer the phone on my 10-minute break. I was advised when I took the job that mail was a priority and the most important job of the day.

The final straw was I had taken Monday off because I didn't feel well. When I came in on Tuesday, mail for the weekend and Monday had not been done; it was stacked on my desk three feet high. I gathered my personal items, turned around, and walked out. I never returned. I called the man I had been talking to and explained what I had done. He reassured me that I would be fine and that he would help with my monthly expenses until I either got the job at the insurance company (because I had two other interviews in addition to the manager's interview) or I got another job.

I arrived in my apartment complex parking lot and sat in my car, pondering whether quitting my job without the certainty of a new position was the right decision. As tears of anxiety welled up in my eyes, I looked through my windshield and saw the reddest Cardinal sitting in the bushes in front of me, just looking at me. At that moment, I felt assured that I had made the right choice; something inside me said I had the job. Whenever I see a

Cardinal, I'm reminded of my grandfather, reassuring me that he is there and everything will be okay. Despite this reassurance, I couldn't help but worry due to my anxiety and PTSD. It's hard not to feel anxious. I had gone through two successful phone interviews but still had to wait for that final confirmation call. The wait for the phone to ring and confirm I had secured my dream job was agonizing. A couple of weeks later, I finally received the call: I had the job and would start work on May 5th. I was ecstatic!

Though I landed the job I wanted, the rest of my life was far from perfect. I rode the high of the new job for months, eventually deciding to end things with the man who had been driving me insane with accusations of talking and seeing my ex-boyfriend while he was out of town. He also accused me of misappropriating the money he had sent for expenses during the month I was without paychecks and awaiting income, not to mention his controlling behavior. I cut ties with him, and it took months of blocking and re-blocking various numbers to finally stop him from trying to contact me. He would vanish for a while only to reappear. This cycle continued for a year until I changed my number last year, and it seems he finally got the message.

My job was the sole source of joy in my life and the only positive reinforcement I received. I was achieving all the goals I set for myself and exceeding my manager's expectations. Yet, my heart still skipped a beat every time I heard a Harley drive through the apartment complex parking lot. Every text received stirred hope in the back of my mind that it might be my ex-boyfriend. The same went for every phone call—I always hoped it would be him. There was always that faint glimmer of hope, that little spark of fire.

I had sworn off dating sites completely, especially after the last disaster I encountered. I wasn't looking for anyone. At my new job with the insurance company, I ran into an old friend and made a few new ones while spending time in the building's "smoke room." Since my heartbreak, I have steadily gained weight. My depression was overwhelming, yet I managed to ignore it during the day, thanks to distractions. I was busy with work and the company of those I had a break and lunch with. I didn't have to dwell on it, but in reality, I was thinking about it all the time. I found myself constantly complaining—about my co-workers, my workload, my bills, my daughter, not seeing my son, and how sad my life was. I had turned all the trauma I experienced into a lifestyle, making myself a permanent victim.

It's no wonder I struggled to maintain friendships. This had been my demeanor throughout my adult life, as far back as I could remember. I never had anything positive to say about anything. I claimed to be a realist, but in truth, I was a pessimist. I must be honest with myself; there was no denying it. Of course, I didn't see it then; I never did when it was important and necessary. My realizations always came too late—during my most vulnerable moments when I needed someone to hold me, and there was no one there. My attitude, the way I carried myself, the tone of my voice, and how I spoke without thinking— often being hurtful with my words, even unintentionally— pushed people away without even realizing it. And then, even when made aware of it, I continued, much to my own detriment.

When my boyfriend and I split up back in October of 2014, I was a size 10/12. I wasn't that big and could still look attractive when I made an effort to clean up. However, even after two years of being alone, I hadn't moved on from him. I had gained quite a bit of weight and started to feel terrible about myself. I was now a size 14/16, and even that was getting tight. I hadn't been that size since being with my ex-husband, and I had promised myself back then that I would never let myself get that large again. My depression and self-pity had taken control.

I had been prescribed Ambien because my depression and anxiety were keeping me from sleeping. I would wake up every morning between 3:00 a.m. and 3:30 a.m. After taking it for several months, my routine became to take the medication and head straight to bed because it would knock me out completely, allowing me to sleep soundly. I seldom dream, and on the rare occasions I do, I don't remember them.

Ambien, being such a strong medication, never induced dreams for me, so I'm certain what I experienced wasn't an illusion, dream, or hallucination. Just minutes after lying down with my eyes closed, I started to see a stage with large, oddly hung draped curtains, like stage curtains but arranged in a peculiar pattern—half-hung, half-not—with red rugs and drapes scattered on the floor and hanging in mid-air, demons dancing around, and a blood-red leather tufted chaise lounge in the center of the room, flanked by two matching tall-backed French-style chairs, all with black wood trim. My ex-boyfriend's wife was sitting on the chaise lounge.

She was dressed in a red, skintight leather catsuit that covered her entire body except her head, complemented by hip-high spiked heeled red leather boots. Meanwhile, I was still in my bed (I sleep totally bare), lying on my back with the covers pulled up to my chest, my eyes wide open, clutching the blankets to my neck, barely able to breathe. She had long red nails and was moving up beside my bed, slowly, creeping like some sort of crab, stretching her bony fingers toward my throat as she said, "Let's see how death comes to your house."

I was terrified. I told myself, "This is a dream; wake up! God save me!" and forced myself to snap out of it. The fear struck deep into my core; her words sent chills down my spine, and the look on her face—it/she was determined to harm me right then and there. She meant every word. This encounter wasn't part of a dream—I had somehow entered a mystical realm, an astral plane. At the time, I knew it signified something, but I wasn't sure what. I would soon find out.

I was so frightened that I didn't want to close my eyes and go back to sleep, scared that I would see her again or that she would return from wherever she had come from. She was terrifying; I hadn't felt that kind of fear since I was a small child. I don't even think I was that scared when I was raped. It felt like she was going to drag me to hell. I didn't recognize her initially because her face morphed into other faces a couple of times.

It was only a few months after that unsettling encounter when I received a call around midnight on a Friday night. I was shocked, surprised, excited, and curious as to why he would be calling at such an odd hour, especially since he had been drinking.

Had she left him again? Was he drowning his sorrows in alcohol? And why was he calling me his second choice? I didn't care; I was just glad he was reaching out to me and not someone else.

He called ME!

It felt like prayers were answered, wishes came true, and he realized we belonged together. There I was, caught up in the fantasy of a fifteen-year-old, a mindset stuck due to my trauma and co-dependency.

We talked for an hour and a half on the phone and decided he should come over. We attempted to have sex, but he was so drunk he passed out. The connection between us felt off, lost—even from my perspective. It was as if he had hurt me so much that something had irrevocably changed. Maybe it was the lingering presence of the other women he had been with since we parted—his wife, his recent girlfriend, and whoever else there might have been that I wasn't aware of.

When I inquired about what had happened between him and his wife, I learned that she had died. At the time of her death, he had been involved with another woman. They found her after she had been decomposing for some time, so it was unclear how long she had been deceased. But when he mentioned that his wife had died around the end of October or the beginning of November in 2016, and we were speaking in the summer of 2017, a chill went up my spine. I didn't say anything, but I knew right then that she had paid me a visit on the night she died. She disliked me so much that she made sure to stop by on her way to her afterlife station, attempting to take me with her. I had wished her dead two years prior during my breakup with her husband, and it had come to pass. Be careful what you wish for; our words cast spells; that's why it's called "spelling."

She came to deliver instant karma for what I had wished upon her. Part of my divination involves seeing people who have passed on—I was about to witness my own demise, but the

Divine allowed me to escape from the realm she had pulled me into and protected me. Once again, the Divine was there for me. I thanked the Divine but carried on with my life. My ex-boyfriend and I reconnected for about a week before he left me once again, going back to whatever girlfriend he had before calling me. The same pattern emerged; I should have recognized it, but instead, I returned to pining for him.

When I was working for the insurance company as a temporary employee in 2013, I made a close friend. When I returned as a full-time employee in 2015, we reconnected. In the smoke room, I also made a couple of new friends. These ladies were mostly nice to me, and there was one woman with whom I became closer than my original friend. She and I spent time together outside of the smoke room group, and she even spent money to help me get a new wardrobe after I had lost about 40 lbs., a consequence of mourning my ex-boyfriend for several months. I dropped the weight in a year, which was quick.

Once I started losing, I became obsessed. It wasn't the healthiest way to lose weight, but before I knew it, I was a size four and very happy. I really liked this lady, but I may have upset her when I told her I appreciated everything she had done for me but didn't want her to think I was a charity case. Not long after, things changed between me and the ladies in the smoke room.

You know, when you get a bunch of women together, there's always one who is the odd one out. Growing up and in my young adult years, that was always me, and it was no different in my mid-life adulthood. Women never change; there are always the "mean girls," and they will exist until the end of time. Even in nursing homes, they exist. Betty does not like Sylvia because

Marvin finds her more attractive, even though he has probably hit on every woman in the place and can't perform because his doctor won't give him the little blue pill due to his heart condition. It's the same everywhere.

I decided one year after Valentine's Day that I would quit vaping out of love for myself. I quit cold turkey, and my best friend from this group, who had been my friend longer than she had been friends with anyone else in the group, joined me in quitting for about three days. The other woman I had been close to also joined us. They sat with me in the mornings for about two more days and then just stopped coming to sit with me altogether without sending a text to explain; they just stopped. I never heard from any of them again. No goodbye, no explanation, nothing. This was very hurtful. I had been nothing but kind to those women. I even cried about it.

As always, I internalized the hurt, dissociated, and added to the emotional trauma and pain; this further fueled my depression. Despite the burden, I kept moving forward. I had bills to pay, a living to make, and responsibilities to uphold. I carried the sadness like a load of iron, dragging behind me like a bag of bricks. My posture reflected my internal state—shoulders hunched, head hung low. This had been my demeanor for years, both standing and sitting, a clear sign of being beaten down.

I likened myself to one of those junkyard dogs, the kind that roam with their heads down, too afraid to make eye contact, scavenging for a bone or a scrap of kindness. Looking back, it seems just pitiful. Loneliness was all I knew, spending my spare time alone with my cat, my constant companion. He was my rock, offering comfort when I cried, and I cried a lot. I wallowed in self-pity, always feeling like the victim, misunderstood, and unloved. The darkness enveloped me completely. I could see no way out, and it seemed like nobody noticed. My relationship with my daughter was nonexistent; she stopped talking to me because I signed another year's lease and refused to move in with her and my grandchildren when she had to leave the house she was living in. Every four months, I visited the psychiatrist at the medicine clinic to renew my prescription for psych medication. The psychiatrist seemed indifferent, merely increasing the dosage or adding another medication.

I voiced my struggles, denying any immediate plans for suicide but confessing to thoughts about it and a profound sense of struggling. Functionally, if I am bipolar, it's type II, which is particularly dangerous when in a severe depressive state. Yet, no one seemed concerned for me except myself. I was aware I was spiraling into trouble, recognizing one of my darkest periods, uncertain if there would be light at the end of this tunnel. In my mind's eye, I am nothing more than a blob from the waist down, sitting in bed, staring at my phone in the dark.

I couldn't grasp what was wrong with me, though deep down, I knew it stemmed from trauma, emotional immaturity, and my attitude—I was unlikeable. The women who were supposed to be my friends didn't like me; the two women I worked with in my office didn't like me; the man I was crazy about didn't want me, and I was starting to hate myself even more than usual. I was disgusting, rude, ignorant—all I did was complain, constantly embroiled in drama. I was as sick of myself as everyone else was. It didn't matter whether I was thin or fat; people disliked me. I was the common denominator, so the problem wasn't with others; it was with me. Unbeknownst to me, I was nearing a breaking point, dissociating more rapidly than ever before.

The apartment became darker each day, especially during the winter. I wouldn't even turn the lights on, sitting in the dark with only the flicker of the television changing from scene to scene or commercial to commercial. The only light I kept on, except when necessary, was the light over the stove—just enough to make coffee in the mornings and feed my cat twice a day. My appetite was minimal, so I didn't dirty the kitchen much, and the bathroom didn't require frequent cleaning; after all, it was just me.

The medication made me increasingly lazy—the more depressed I became, the lazier I got, the less I took care of the house, and the less I took care of myself. I just didn't care anymore—about anything. However, I made sure to keep my work life impeccable. You might have noticed something was off by my appearance or demeanor, but my work ethic and output never faltered. I had some issues with my attitude toward a colleague, but other than that, I was like a functioning alcoholic, maintaining a façade so no one could tell I had any problems concerning my work. Even though I wasn't meeting anyone in the mornings, I still arrived an hour early, sitting in the building and scrolling through my phone.

Why? I had nowhere else to be. It was routine, I suppose—I didn't want to be late, wanted a good parking spot, and wanted to get a jump on the day. I spent breaks and lunches alone as well. I thought that once I lost weight, I would put myself back out there and find someone. Being thin, I believed, would solve all my problems. I saw my weight, my looks, and my age as the only barriers to finding the love of my life. While I couldn't change my age, I had managed to lose weight, and I could enhance my looks with makeup (after all, I was once considered attractive). However, I didn't have anyone to go out with.

My daughter had quit drinking and had settled down, now in her late 30s. I had no friends and lacked the confidence to go out alone, so I spent my time at home, a habit that had become second nature. I saw my son every six to eight weeks for a two-hour dinner, usually initiated by me. We compared diet notes, tips, and tricks for conversation, but we had nothing in common.

I felt forgotten, just like in my childhood, unsure if it was my own doing, the circumstances of my life, or how my children truly felt about me. Perhaps I had secluded myself. When my daughter began talking to me again, she would occasionally invite me over to her house or her friend's house for cookouts, but I didn't care for the company she kept, so I never attended. So, to a certain extent, I guess I did isolate myself.

I didn't have any hobbies of my own. I had spent no time investing in myself to discover who I was, what I was interested in (independent of someone else's interests), what I liked (not just what someone else liked), and what my tastes were (not just someone else's preferences) because I had always morphed into what someone else wanted in a partner, never truly being myself. So, I am still discovering all the wonderful things about myself. I'm hoping to find out that I have talents I never knew I had— maybe I'll discover activities I always wanted to try but didn't think I could excel at, only to find out I am great at them!

Chapter 11: Self-Reflection and Renewal

"Do to others as you would have them do to you."
—Luke Chapter 27, Verse 31

I had begun to pray at night, speaking to the Divine, asking for blessings for my children, for the women who had turned their backs on me, and for the family that had abandoned me. I tried not to ask for things for myself. I was always taught to pray for others and not for myself; I also believed it was highly selfish to pray for oneself that one should sacrifice one's needs or desires for others.

I was led to believe that martyrdom was a heroic act; giving your life for someone else was presented as the greatest act of love. "All for one and one for all!" This mindset prevented me from letting go of the emotional attachment to those I felt obligated to because I was supposed to love them more than myself. Thus, I believed I needed to sacrifice for them—my wealth, happiness, fortune, love, relationships, body, health, home, and emotional well-being. However, I came to realize that this belief is not true. This is co-dependency – narcissists use this tactic.

No one should have to sacrifice those things, or anything, for anyone. Love is not about sacrifice or martyrdom. My mother and the Catholic Church taught me incorrectly. The narrative of the Divine sacrificing His only Son, Jesus, and Jesus sacrificing Himself out of love for all hindered me from loving myself and knowing my authentic self all my life. You should never sacrifice yourself or your feelings for anybody or anything. Be your true self, your Higher Self, and never sacrifice who you truly are. Stand in your power and speak your truth at all times, whether it is popular or not. Be true to yourself and follow your heart.

I made a deal with the Divine that if my children were given their Soulmates, I would give up on meeting mine—a sacrifice for my children. I realize now that bargaining in prayers, tinkering with Karma, or attempting to influence Divine manifestations are not only regrettable but also dangerous. I have changed my mind about making that deal; I learned that one should not try to make bargains with the Divine, nor should anyone dabble in someone else's energy without permission.

This was proven to me through my experience with my ex-boyfriend's wife. I couldn't shake the incident from my mind; for weeks after her afterlife visit, when I went to bed, I would think about it and be afraid to close my eyes for fear she might appear again.

It was around the spring of 2018 when I received an unexpected text. Surprise, surprise! It was from my ex-boyfriend. He was inquiring about my well-being and what I had been up to. Having recently ended another relationship, he confessed he had missed me and expressed a desire to see me. Despite being foolish, extremely lonely, and for some inexplicable reason still in love with him, I acquiesced. At the time, I was looking the best I had in years—thin, healthy, and financially stable. However, he didn't appear as well as the last time I had seen him; he was missing a couple of teeth and looked significantly older, as if life had been harsh and he had spent too much time exposed to the elements.

There was a palpable awkwardness between us. I could sense his discomfort, which was warranted given how he had treated me over the four years we had known each other. I had always treated him with love and kindness, and he was aware of that. Conversely, he had, on multiple occasions, treated me with disrespect, inconsiderate, and unkindness. He confessed that he regretted not choosing me when he had the chance and claimed to have learned from his mistakes, insisting that this time he was back for good.

I wanted to believe him—desperately.

I feared losing him again, worried that it wasn't real, that I was dreaming (and indeed, I was—my intuition was correct once again). It seemed too good to be true, and it was. He had invited me to a concert that weekend, and he was planning to take his bike due to the favorable weather. However, since our last conversation on Wednesday that week, I haven't heard from him. He wasn't responding to my texts, and my instincts warned me I wouldn't be attending the concert, considering all the times he had let me down since kicking me out of his house in 2014. So, I didn't bother getting ready.

As expected, the time he was supposed to pick me up came and went without any communication from him. I can't recall if it was a few days later, but he eventually called to apologize, explaining he had opted to go to a bar with some biker friends instead, which was why he stood me up.

He had become a rude, inconsiderate, mean asshole—someone completely opposite of the man I had known years ago. When we tried to be intimate, I found myself incapable of having intercourse with him due to inadequate moisture, making it extremely painful. I assume this was because he was in such a hurry there was no time for proper preparation. I was extremely nervous, as it had been a long time since we had been together, and I hadn't been intimate in years.

Moreover, he was different—rough, almost cruel. I'm not sure who he had been with, but they must have tolerated rough treatment. The thought of being with this version of him—this man obsessed only with his own arousal, taking testosterone pills he received in the mail, all juiced up—was unappealing. This, combined with his current personality and attitude toward me and women in general, led me to decide that if I never heard from him again, it would not matter anymore.

I have not felt the same about him since that day. Occasionally, I would feel a twinge of the old affection for him, perhaps the "what could have been" feeling that surfaces now and then. I know that he is not the one for me; the Divine has made that quite clear. I think the reason I gave him so many chances was my co-dependency, a trait I learned from my mother.

She gave my father a chance after chance, woman after woman, so I let him back into my life time and time again until I finally learned my lesson. My mother, on the other hand, never really learned hers; she would still take him back today if he were still alive and single. This realization has also been made quite clear to me. Each day, the Divine is making things clearer to me. That was the last time I heard from him. He never contacted me again. On Facebook, I saw some postings about him getting engaged but never marrying. I also saw a posting from one of his nephews regarding the anniversary of his mother's passing, leading me to assume she died during the pandemic. I feel sorry for him because my intuition tells me he has never taken the time to truly grieve for his wife or to deal with his lingering feelings for her. He has jumped into relationships without properly healing from the heartbreak of previous ones. Trust me, as someone who has lived that lifestyle, I can attest it doesn't work; it doesn't solve the problems or cure the emotional trauma and psychological damage.

He likely hasn't properly grieved for his mother, either. More than likely, what he needs is someone just to hold him and let him cry for hours if necessary. I know I need that myself. I believe that kind of therapy would be an incredible healing tool for many people and could even help bring the world closer together. I'm sure the idea isn't new, but now, more than ever, is the time to implement this method of healing.

In 2019, I purchased my own home. I was so proud and happy to have my own place—no co-owner, no co-signer—a $100,000 home that was all mine! I had accomplished it all on my own. At 57 years old, with a mortgage set for a thirty-year loan, I wasn't sure how I was going to pay for the home over the next 30 years, but I had bought a house. This was a dream that became a reality in just ninety days; I received loan approval for $100,000, found a realtor, picked out a home, made a bid, signed a contract, and closed on the house—all within ninety days. It was the fulfillment of a wish, a manifestation turned into reality. As always, I thought a change of scenery and buying something new would alter my circumstances, shift my outlook, and change my thought patterns; I believed it would fix things overnight. I am finally realizing (maturing) that nothing is fixed overnight or with a pill. It takes work—usually constant, everyday effort. Anything worth having, changing, or incorporating into your life requires hard work. People always told me that negative self-talk and negative talk about my life would breed negativity in my life. Deep down, I knew they were right and understood it to be true, yet I continued to engage in it, not realizing the real damage I was doing until later. Learning this was an extremely hard lesson.

I was alone in the house for almost a year when the pandemic struck. My daughter, who had been leasing to own a home, found herself in a difficult situation as her relationship fell apart. She was moving out just two days before rent was due and, with the pandemic escalating, found herself without anywhere to go.

Naturally, with a three-bedroom house, I opened my doors to her and my two grandchildren. She took over my house, brought her two large dogs, stored her belongings in my garage (which didn't fit in two storage units), started making the rules, and disregarded every rule I set, everything I said or did. We triggered each other terribly; in truth, we always had.

It was worse now because she had worked on herself after learning a lot about psychology in college and had begun her Spiritual Awakening Journey, perhaps without fully realizing it, making significant progress. The problem was she began analyzing everyone, trying to dictate how they should "fix" themselves, insisting on her way because she deemed it best. She was hyper-focused on me—laser-centered—and for some reason, she had me in her sights and was relentless.

She is a bully, labeling her behavior as being assertive; she stands up, waves her arms around, and paces the floor, describing herself as "animated." When she gets angry and yells (and calls others out for it), she claims she's just being "passionate." She has a justification for every negative aspect of her personality and her unruly behavior, insisting that if you are intimidated by her, the issue lies with you—not her. According to her, if you're perceived as weaker, timid, or unable to defend yourself, you are the problem, not her. This viewpoint is highly narcissistic.

Things would seem okay; months could pass without incident. Then, seemingly out of nowhere, something would trigger me—a financial strain, a bad day at work (despite working from home three days a week), or simply the fact that she lived in my home for $400 a month. This rent covered two rooms, insurance for her vehicles, monthly bills for two phones, laundry privileges, storage, gas, water, electricity, cable, internet, paper and cleaning products, and lighters—I couldn't keep enough lighters around; she had a knack for taking them, even if they weren't hers.

The house expenses totaled approximately $2,000, so it's clear I bore the brunt of the expenses, not including my personal costs. Yet, I was constantly told she was paying more than enough for rent and utilities, a point I vehemently disagreed with. Money had always been a contentious issue between us. I was always lending financial support, which she never acknowledged. She complained I never helped her, insisting she had to manage everything on her own.

Meanwhile, she was saving considerable amounts of money. She had amassed about $17,000 and was spending it on dental work, contemplating a breast augmentation, purchasing a new bed, buying herself a Harley, acquiring her first brand-new car, and spending hundreds on tattoos. My frustration grew as I worried about potentially losing my home while she seemingly spent frivolously, contributing only $400 a month to our shared expenses. This disparity bred deep resentment within me.

As I have mentioned, she conveniently forgets about the insurance money from my car accident, the extra funds from consolidation loans, and cash withdrawals from credit cards. I could elaborate further, but I choose not to. Unlike my daughter, I have never financially supported my son, as he has never asked for anything, even in times of desperate need.

There was a moment when, over dinner, I inquired if he owned clothes other than those he was wearing, as they were all I had ever seen on him. His response was no, so I took him to JC Penney. His gratitude was immense as if I had bought him a gold watch—a stark contrast to my daughter's expectations when I took her shopping. Now that he has financial stability and is dating a dentist, his attitude has shifted to resemble hers, behaving as if he is too good for me.

Before my daughter and grandchildren moved in, my house was immaculate. I've always been a clean freak, detesting clutter and misplaced items. I believe everything has a place and should be kept there when not in use. Nothing irritates me more than seeing items out of place or dirty rooms that guests might see. My daughter's homes always had laundry in the living room— clean but awaiting folding and storage. This habit drove me insane! I established a rule that upon her moving in, there should be no laundry in the living room. This rule was adhered to for merely three days. Her living spaces were constantly cluttered and dirty. I had mandated no dirty dishes in the sink for days to avoid attracting roaches, a rule she ignored from the outset. Within a year, I constantly sprayed, dusted, and sought ways to exterminate the pervasive bugs that had invaded my bedroom, bathroom, and beyond. I was fed up with their presence and made my feelings abundantly clear, which she resented. She detested my blunt honesty, especially when it was delivered in anger, often after we had been screaming at each other.

Our arguments would escalate, jumping from one issue to another. Exhausted by the filth and disorder, I refused to emulate my mother by tirelessly cleaning up after them. They were perfectly capable of tidying up after themselves. However, the house only received a thorough cleaning when I undertook the task myself, typically during their annual trips to the river around July 4 or, if possible, during the Christmas holidays.

I would dedicate one of my four days to cleaning the shared areas from top to bottom, then spraying and dusting for bugs. The cleanliness would only last for the two days I was home alone, but it was nice to have my old home back, even if just for a short while.

We frequently argued about the constant state of filth and clutter in the house, making it seem futile to clean since it would still appear dirty regardless. She would provocatively tell me to get off my "fat ass" and clean, asserting that I was just as capable as she was. She argued that her kids did their part by doing the dishes and managing their laundry (once a month); therefore, I didn't think it was too much to ask for them to clean the bathroom, sweep, and mop, especially considering they were living in my house, which I expected to be kept clean.

After all, I paid the mortgage and supplemented the monthly household expenses. I refused to be exploited and treated like my mother was by my little sister. I was not going to act as both the provider and the cleaner for her and her untidy habits.

When you are guests in someone else's house, you should adapt to their way of living—if they are clean, you live clean, too! It's about keeping your room tidy and maintaining cleanliness in their house, especially in their kitchen. You don't take over and live as you do in your own home. It's a matter of common sense, courtesy, and respect—all of which I received none. Moreover, my cats were in perfect health before she and her two large dogs moved in.

Cats can easily become stressed, leading to quick deterioration in their health. Following the dogs' arrival, both of my cats developed serious chronic conditions: my male developed thyroid disease and my female suffered from chronic kidney and bladder infections, resulting in her urinating all over the house due to stress. Eventually, my male cat passed away, but my female hasn't had any issues since they moved out.

My relationship with my granddaughter was somewhat better than with my daughter; we could communicate more civilly. She had more patience with me than my daughter ever did. My daughter treated me as if I were a four-year-old struggling to articulate, repeating the same two words without ever making a point. She seemed disinterested in anything I had to say or any questions I wanted to ask, dismissing them as stupid or ridiculous. It felt as though she had no time for what she perceived as my silliness. I reached a point of frustration where I just wanted her disrespectful self out of my house.

I longed for her to take her glib, rude, inconsiderate, disrespectful, unempathetic, narcissistic, and bitchy demeanor far away from me. She was perpetually in a bad mood, reacting negatively to anything said to her, regardless of its nature. Her attitude was so foul that my grandchildren had learned to assess her mood instantly; they would immediately retreat to their bedroom if she returned from work with a foul temper. This survival strategy against her tantrums and mental and emotional abuse seemed ingrained in them from a young age, a realization I came too late to salvage our relationship. Whenever she began criticizing something I had said or done, I would withdraw to my room, only for her to follow and resume her haranguing. It was exhausting.

Her bullying matched or surpassed that of my mother. She leveraged my guilt over her troubled childhood against me, a hallmark of narcissistic manipulation. Unable to get what she wanted through direct means—she expected me to raise her children as my mother had done for my little sister—she resorted to guilt and manipulation for financial benefit and to inflict emotional and mental punishment as her form of retribution. Despite these challenges, I will always keep the door open for both of my children to join me in therapy to mend our relationships. I am more than willing to collaborate on healing because I genuinely desire to heal, unlike my mother, who wasn't even willing to try.

I hadn't been dating at all while my daughter was trying to move on from a man she had been with for the past three years. She ventured into the world of dating sites for the first time and began meeting men outside her usual circle, exploring a wide array of potential partners. It was refreshing to see her taking an interest in new people—embracing changes, new experiences, and places, all of which seemed promising for her future. Remarkably, she had abstained from alcohol for nearly two years and had been clean from drugs for fifteen years.

I was genuinely proud of her achievements. She started arranging casual meetings for coffee or drinks (despite not drinking alcohol herself) with some of these men, and a few connections lasted a couple of months before she experienced ghosting. It's perplexing how common it has become for people to abruptly cease all communication without any explanation.

She met a man from out of state, and despite her initial reluctance to engage in a long-distance relationship, they began texting and talking. They saw each other regularly for a couple of months, but the relationship faced numerous challenges. During this period, our relationship became strained. We argued about her new boyfriend, her job situation, finances, and living arrangements, among other issues. Yet, she sought my advice regarding this man.

Despite my reservations, I hesitated to express them fully, fearing she would label me as a "Debbie Downer" or a "Negative Nelly"—accusing me of always seeing the negative side or being jealous because I was single. She believed my intuition skewed towards the negative, thus dismissing my advice. Consequently, I kept most of my opinions to myself.

I've never understood why she asks for my opinion when she tends to dismiss my ideas or opinions as either ignorant or merely echoing her own thoughts. What's the point of approaching me in the first place? I've been baffled by this dynamic most of the time, by our entire relationship, to be honest. The mixed signals she sends are so reminiscent of my mother. She has even mentioned feeling like the parent in our relationship. Reflecting on this, I must admit that I often felt like a young child, as if I weren't truly an adult but rather an emotional teenager trapped in an older person's body. This sense of youthful insecurity wasn't just confined to personal interactions; it extended to job interviews, meetings with doctors and nurses, and interactions with employers, coworkers, and even friends. I constantly felt as though everyone else was in a position of authority over me, leaving me perpetually in the role of the child.

This realization compelled me to explore what experiences in my current or past lives might have affected my Inner Child, locking me into this state of emotional immaturity. Identifying the root cause allowed me to acknowledge and thank my Higher Self for bringing these insights to my attention. I learned to move with the flow of emotions tied to those memories or situations and then release them. Although it might seem like a repetitive process, as I've mentioned before, the journey is ongoing. Our Higher Self continues to reveal aspects of our Shadow Selves, necessitating constant reflection and growth.

My daughter's relationship with me mirrored that of my mother and me in many ways. I remained the abused child, with my daughter stepping into the role of my mother and becoming my abuser, albeit not physically. The abuse was slower and more emotional, yet she seemed to feel I deserved it. The significant difference between my relationship with my daughter and that with my mother is that I harbored a desire to punish my mother, which I eventually did by making no contact.

My daughter, on the other hand, actively sought to punish me throughout our relationship. My mother never truly experienced my wrath unless one considers my years of absence as such. However, I view wrath as a form of vicious revenge, repeatedly inflicted, which doesn't align with merely distancing myself from her life. My daughter has erased me from her life as I have my mother. Yet, she took it further by belittling me, exploiting my low self-esteem and self-worth, and making me feel inferior for not having or not being able to improve these aspects of myself.

She seemed to adopt the disdainful view her father and stepmother had of me—a misguided, worthless individual who had somehow entrapped her father into marriage and produced a "devil child." Moreover, like my mother, she wielded conditional love as a weapon. We were fine as long as I was financially generous or compliant with her wishes, regardless of any inconvenience it caused others. But the moment I said no or posed an inconvenience to her, she would withdraw her affection, treating me as if I were "dead to her."

The one distinction between these two relationships was that my daughter and I once shared a close bond, being best friends in addition to our familial ties—a dynamic we probably should have reconsidered.

We always had each other's back. There was a time when she would boast about me and express her gratitude. When her friends left her side, I was the constant, the one she turned to for support, financial help, or a ride from jail or a bar. However, she never confided her deepest, darkest secrets in me, utilizing my presence primarily when she found herself devoid of other listeners or in need of assistance.

Facing the truth about oneself and those who were supposed to love you is challenging. I acknowledge that I may have disappointed my children, which is something many parents do, but I'm not convinced that my actions warrant a no-contact situation. However, that decision isn't mine to make; it's based on my children's feelings, not mine.

I've given them their space, and if I never hear from them again, I have to accept that as possibly being part of the Divine's plan. Regardless of how I feel, they believe their decision is justified, and I must respect their boundaries, choices, and feelings. I expect the same level of respect from my mother, siblings, and anyone else with my choice.

The man my daughter became involved with in a neighboring state was not who he presented himself to be. He was an evil, controlling, and manipulating narcissist. He deceived her about serious health issues, exploited her emotionally and mentally, and was simultaneously involved with other women.

Despite the clear warning signs, she continued the relationship. During this period, our relationship was in turmoil. Desperate to catch him in the act of cheating—to prove a point— she moved to his home state, which was a two-hour drive from her job in our city, resulting in a four-hour round trip each day for several months. She neglected her children, centering her entire world around this man.

She spent Thanksgiving and Christmas with him instead of with her children, only spending a couple of hours on Christmas Eve with them before returning to him. It was as if she were under his "spell."

Thankfully, she was divinely protected during this time despite being in a harmful situation.

Chapter 12: Frayed Edges of Reality

I worked as a legal secretary for a bankruptcy attorney at a large firm downtown from October 2021 to May 2022. During Mother's Day weekend, I fractured my back. This job hadn't been a good fit, mainly because I had no training in that specific area of law.

Later, around October 2022, I found another full-time position at a law firm. Initially, I did not realize this job would lead me to retire, marking the start of my journey toward abundance and financial security. It also began my long-awaited and needed spiritual awakening.

Just two months into this job, the paralegal who had been with the firm for thirty-six years resigned to work elsewhere. This departure should have been a significant warning sign to me, and indeed, it became apparent a few weeks later. A month later, the firm dismissed the other support staff, leaving me to manage all support duties alone. They did not hire anyone new for at least thirty days, possibly longer.

By April, I was overwhelmed. The attorney, who was formerly a judge, had irked me from the start. His demeanor suggested he was smarter and better, believing he knew my job more than I did, despite my thirty years of experience as a legal assistant/secretary. It was frustrating to deal with someone who only cared about the end product without understanding the effort involved in producing it. Our personalities clashed terribly, akin to combining pickles and jelly. He could not stand me, and the feeling was mutual. Whenever I needed something or questioned a procedure, he complained to the senior attorney about me. He would enter the senior attorney's office and close the door, leaving me hesitant to disturb him for the rest of the day. This routine hindered our work, causing delays. I would fall behind, and his frustration with me would grow.

When I began, the physical filing was already a year behind and continued to pile up. Despite my daily responsibilities, I was expected to keep up with this growing backlog. It became an increasingly heavy burden, and his frustration with my performance only intensified.

The senior partner was somewhat more relaxed about things, but he shared the same level of frustration. He couldn't grasp why everything was lagging. He simply didn't understand why I couldn't keep up and why tasks were falling behind. Initially, I was the sole person in the office responsible for all support staff duties. Without a receptionist, another secretary, assistant, or paralegal, I was the only support tasked with everything. Yet, the expectation was that nothing should fall behind. This situation left me angry, frustrated and stressed, and my anxiety was sky-high!

They decided to hire a bookkeeper but did not bring on a paralegal or another secretary. Two months later, they finally hired a paralegal. By that point, I was struggling to keep up, so overwhelmed that I could barely manage the basics. Docketing, handling the daily mail, faxes, and emails, and opening new files were all I could keep up with. Everything else was neglected. The situation was deteriorating. They were becoming increasingly aggravated, and my frustration was mounting. Things looked bleak for me; I feared they would terminate my employment at any moment. Despite my efforts, I couldn't keep pace. My misery deepened with each passing day. The thirty-minute commute to and from work became a daily ordeal. I loathed the people I worked with, the cramped 3x5 workspace, the office atmosphere, and even its smell. Desperately wanting to leave, I nonetheless needed the job.

Compounding this workplace misery was the weight of depression from the last forty-five years, the loneliness, and years of guilt, shame, and trauma pressing down on me. This burden had been building, intensifying over the past seven years, and becoming especially unbearable in the last three. The pressure was immense, yet I couldn't pinpoint the cause. I yearned for a change, exhausted from feeling this way.

I longed to experience joy, happiness, and the sound of laughter. Everywhere I looked, I saw only depression. I tried to engage my grandchildren in conversation, aiming to forge some connection with them. My granddaughter and I shared some meaningful conversations during those last months, from October 2022 to March 2023.

Depression was widespread in my household; even my cats seemed affected. One cat was confined to my bedroom all day because she would attack my granddaughter's cat. This situation lasted a whole year, leaving her sad from her "jail" time, only allowed to roam the house for eight hours at night. My male cat suffered from thyroid disease, gradually deteriorating until I had to lay him to rest in November 2023. The atmosphere at home felt like a cold dungeon. I had to confront the reality that it had been dark, gloomy, and sad for the three years my daughter and grandchildren lived with me. Truthfully, my life had been bleak for over 40 years, culminating in a sensation of the walls closing in, with the water rising to my nostrils; I was drowning. I couldn't decide if I had been more miserable and depressed during the first year I lived alone or the last three years surrounded by family. My mental health had suffered—the stress from losing my job at the insurance company, the toll of the pandemic, and the anxiety of finding steady work for several years had left me teetering on the edge.

I kept my struggle hidden from my household. We had our arguments over the years, and I would retreat to my room to sulk. Sometimes, I'd spend days there, emerging only to grab something to drink or eat—food I had bought for myself and stashed away. I did this because I felt uncomfortable using the groceries they provided for anything I might enjoy.

Occasionally, I would order food for delivery, always making sure to include everyone at home. Despite accusations of ordering food just for myself, I always ensured there was something for my grandchildren and my daughter when she was around. I spent a considerable amount of money on them, but my contributions never seemed to be appreciated.

My life had become a nightmare. I was essentially just existing in my own home. My accommodations were limited to a room with a toilet and a sink. My two cats and I spent most of our time in this room, except when I ventured into the living room to clean my smoke or enjoy the rare moments when the grandchildren were in their shared room, she was away or occupied in the garage with a project that seemed to drag on indefinitely. However, the moment someone entered the living room, I would retreat to my bedroom for the rest of the evening.

I stopped watching television because my enjoyment of my favorite shows was consistently disrupted. Whenever I was watching something, my daughter would invariably enter the room, ask, "Are you watching this?" and then proceed to question why I was on my phone if I said yes. Frustrated, I would relent and let her change the channel, even though she would be on her phone within ten minutes. It felt like a constant double standard. This pattern of conceding mirrored my entire life, where I felt unable to assert my preferences or opinions, even in my own home, using my own television. "I pay the electric bill," I would think, echoing words I had heard from my mother. It dawned on me that I was repeating her words, but the reality was that my daughter had taken over my entire house.

I must confess I was physically scared of her. I had witnessed her confront three women at once and emerge as the sole person standing. I had seen her stand up to her ex-boyfriend, a man over six feet tall and weighing more than two hundred pounds, without backing down. When we argued, she would threaten me with physical harm, getting in my face so close our noses almost touched. But you dared not do the same to her, or she would retaliate physically. With her, it was always a double standard; she could say or do anything, but I couldn't dare to challenge her.

This dynamic was eerily reminiscent of my relationship with my mother. I allowed my daughter to treat me in the same way, driven by the same fear I had felt towards my mother. She berated me, making me feel guilty for lacking self-esteem, self-worth, and self-confidence. I felt guilty and ashamed because I lacked the skills to "repair" my self-worth, self-confidence, and self-esteem. She made me feel worthless, just like my mother did, albeit for different reasons. Yet, the outcome was the same: it was still abusive behavior that inflicted the same kind of trauma.

My daughter was right; she had become the mother in our relationship, essentially stepping into my mother's shoes in every aspect. The only difference was she hadn't physically assaulted me, though she had threatened to, especially when I said something that struck a nerve or was too close to the truth.

Over the past four years, she couldn't hide her true feelings towards me. These feelings became glaringly apparent when I moved out with my last boyfriend due to an eviction, leaving her with a house full of items and nowhere to go. The situation worsened when she wanted to move in with me while I was living in my apartment, and I refused. This refusal marked a significant turning point in our relationship. She declared that I was dead to her, a statement that held until she needed to move in with me in 2020. Despite her moving in, our relationship continued to deteriorate.

She would only approach me or call when she needed something, or I would visit during birthdays or holidays if they were home. But the distance between us grew after I had said no to her for the first time since she was a child, and she began to punish me for it. My granddaughter later confirmed the resentment and the punitive distance that had been festering since then after a particularly revealing conversation following an argument between my daughter and me. As I've come to realize, my daughter harbored resentment and meted out her vengeance in subtle yet hurtful ways, starting from when she was thirteen years old. It all began with a phone call, during which she told me she didn't want to come home from her father's house. Since then, she has taken every opportunity to jab at me, a pattern I'm only now recognizing as I look back.

Her decision to block me on social media and cut off contact represents her ultimate stance in rejecting our relationship, essentially protesting against me being her mother. However, as much as it may dismay both of my children, I am their mother. Regardless of whether they like it, dislike it, love it, or hate it, they have to accept this truth and move forward. It's a part of our lives, a slice of our history. Life can be harsh, indeed.

I had to come to terms with my mother, whether I liked it or not. Now, it's your turn to accept me. We don't have to pick our parents, but we must acknowledge that they are our parents, and without them, we wouldn't exist. My daughter doesn't like either of her parents. She detests her father and loathes her mother. It seems we're in the same boat now, aren't we? However, I've learned to forgive, enabling me to move forward truly. Forgiveness is essential for progressing on this Spiritual Awakening Journey towards abundance and your highest good.

I don't believe it's possible to embark on this journey, to understand what you genuinely desire, and to manifest those desires without first forgiving everyone who has hurt or abused you, forgiving yourself, and learning to love those people and yourself. Only then can you transition into a new dimension or astral plane.

I pray that she will find her true Spiritual Awakening Journey and discover the genuine path it entails. This journey isn't just about Tarot readings communicating with ancestors or those who have passed away, although these practices can open the channel to your Spirit Guides and Angels. For me, the real journey began with delving inward to connect with my Inner Child, healing my emotional trauma, and connecting with my Higher Self.

This is the Christ connection, which reestablished my connection with the Divine. We are the Temple of the Divine, housing our Higher Self. This temple is where the Higher Self worships the Divine, the creator of all living things. This sacred space within you is where you should worship; the connection between the Divine and Christ resides within you.

My daughter ended a long-distance relationship she was in; it had turned into a perilous spiritual situation for her, sparking my own Spiritual Awakening Journey. She received communication from a spirit guiding her through her journey due to the extreme danger she faced—physical, emotional, mental, and incredibly spiritual. The message, which appeared on her phone during one of her lengthy commutes, congratulated her for transcending, stating she had ascended.

Shortly after receiving this message, she returned home following many months of near-fatal accidents, car crashes, health issues (she's diabetic), and financial troubles—essentially, a streak of bad luck. Her emotional state was erratic, oscillating between excitement, confusion, fear, exhilaration, and worry. It was as though she was experiencing a whirlwind of emotions all at once. I found myself captivated by her story as she tried to make sense of what was happening.

She shared suspicions about other women, particularly one she was convinced her partner was seeing, despite lacking concrete proof. Discoveries revealed he had lied about having a severe medical condition, a revelation that was both unsurprising yet hard to fathom. I had harbored doubts about this man from the start, but given the often strained nature of our relationship, I chose to remain silent. She later learned about the women he had been communicating with since the beginning of their two-year relationship. Despite these revelations, her stay was temporary, as she had purchased a home that was soon to close.

She had always vowed to buy a home far from the city, away from the town where she grew up, to distance herself from a past abusive relationship and others she had left behind, including me, as I still reside in that city. She maintained that once she left, she would never return, as nothing here held value for her; it seemed she had forgotten about me.

Nevertheless, she achieved what she had set her mind to. I am proud of her. Owning a real home was significant for her, having never had a permanent place to call home. We moved frequently during her childhood, and she felt out of place in the homes of her parents. Signing the papers for her own home was a dream realized. I was genuinely happy for her on that day, filled with excitement.

She left at the beginning of May 2023, and I found myself alone in my home again, just over a year from the day she moved in when COVID struck. The silence in the house was deafening despite all the living room furniture being in place, except for the large cat tree. The emptiness echoed loudly, with only two bedrooms unfurnished—one serving as a storage space for litter boxes and the other remaining closed off. Reacquainting myself with the spacious bathroom felt so strange. Despite it being summer, the house felt cold, prompting me to set the thermostat to 76 degrees.

Throughout her stay, my daughter often lectured me about my low self-esteem and how I should "fix" it through self-care. She believed I didn't need therapy but should focus on improving my physical well-being. She encouraged me to journal, meditate, wear makeup again, tend to my nails, and get pedicures—all forms of self-care. She insisted that positive thinking and avoiding negative self-talk would transform my life. Perhaps this was the moment to embark on my journey. I had long said I needed time without any responsibilities, without anyone living with me—just time for me to focus on myself. Now, the Divine had provided me with this opportunity; it was now or never.

I knew changes were necessary; I had been aware of this since my twenties but had chosen to ignore it. Now, I was at a point where ignoring it was no longer an option. Our "discussions" about this invariably ended with me in tears.

Couldn't she see what she was doing? She was merely triggering me. Did she not realize that she was the trigger, and perhaps she should examine her actions and stop? Instead, she blamed me for being triggered, not acknowledging her role in causing these reactions. How was this supposed to help?

This pattern resembled the cycle of abuse I experienced with my mother: she would criticize me for something I couldn't do, which would upset me, leading to further criticism for my reaction, spiraling into more distress because I couldn't calm down. The cycle was relentless; it just did not stop! She told me I needed to confront my Shadow Self—to acknowledge that I couldn't heal without doing so. She emphasized the importance of integrating my Shadow Self with my Higher Self and Inner Child. Healing my Inner Child and forgiving my mother were essential steps. Despite her staunch defense of my mother, claiming she did the best she could with the knowledge she had from her own upbringing, her empathy seemed to extend only to her.

"Have some empathy," she would insist. Yet, when it came to me, her empathy vanished; I was held to a different standard. According to her, the reasons or excuses that applied to my mother did not apply to me. I was labeled abusive and accused of mistreating my children, while my mother was seen merely as a victim of her circumstances.

I was told that I, on the other hand, needed a Spiritual Awakening Journey. It was crucial that I embark on this journey now. It promised enlightenment, healing, and peace—seemingly the solution I had been searching for to draw me out of my darkness and into the light, a path to discover the truth and my purpose. My attraction to this journey stemmed from different reasons than hers. Initially, I sought emotional and spiritual healing, with mental healing following suit. She, however, was drawn to it as an escape from the web of deception she found herself entangled in.

In April 2023, I started following several Tarot readers on a social media platform, paying attention to their readings. My daughter claimed those were "her readings," even though most Tarot readers aim their guidance at the "collective"—drawing from a broad spectrum of energies rather than focusing on an individual. Typically, personal readings require private sessions with the reader.

I gradually began to test my Higher Self and the Divine, exploring whether any messages from those Tarot readings were meant for me. I looked for Angel numbers in the messages, on clocks at the times I received them, on my dashboard mileage, and in the number of likes, saves, or comments on these messages. Sometimes I found Angel numbers, and sometimes I didn't. I learned to embrace what resonated with me and to disregard what didn't.Things at the office were deteriorating rapidly. They had hired a paralegal, but by then, my enthusiasm for the job had waned entirely. I had been contemplating leaving for months. The sole reasons keeping me there were the necessity of earning a living and the financial stability it provided.

I had grown to loathe the office, my colleagues, and the entire work environment—I desperately wanted out. That Friday, I went home with the heavy thought of returning to work on Monday looming over me. Over the weekend, I attempted to unwind, but I hadn't really started to work on my actual journey. My activities were limited to listening and watching Tarot readings, seeking insights into my life, and planning my next steps.

Meanwhile, my daughter was gradually moving her belongings into her new home. Since she had moved some distance away, she would bring my grandchildren to the city for their dental appointments. I would take them, allowing the children to do their laundry, while she gathered a few necessities before returning home in the evening. On several occasions, we discussed her desire to leave her job and embark on a self-employment venture in the spiritual field, aiming for an early retirement. Now, she is only 42, and I am 61—logically, I should be the one retiring.

However, that was beside the point.

When I mentioned exploring opportunities on a social media site, her reaction was explosive. She accused me of jealousy and imitation, urging me to find my own path and to stop encroaching on her interests. Unbeknownst to her, my sisters had been practicing Tarot readings and witchcraft long before she was born, and my interest in witchcraft dated back many years before her birth. She wasn't the pioneer of these practices, and through our family lineage, she wasn't the first to engage in them either.

I woke up that Monday morning with no intention of resigning from my job. As I sat in the office parking lot, I browsed through my emails and social media apps, where I stumbled upon a Tarot reading. The message from the Tarot reader spoke about doing what feels right and following the guidance from the Spirit (which I equate with the Divine). Suddenly, the thought crossed my mind: *'You need to leave this job. It's not serving your highest good.'*

My immediate worry was, "I can't afford to leave this job; I don't have another one lined up."

Then, as if in response, I heard, "What did I just tell you?"

Chapter 13: Journey to Inner Awakening

Upon entering the office, I spent the morning seeking confirmation from the Universe (the Divine) about the Angel numbers I kept seeing. I told myself if quitting my job was the right decision, I needed a sign.

Then, I looked at my phone: 8:08; I kept asking if it was right. I looked at it and looked at it a couple of minutes later, 8:28; then, 8:48 — the pattern continued throughout the morning.

I was astounded and thought, "This can't be real," yet I was also growing nervous. My boss hadn't arrived yet, and I hoped to leave before noon. At the same time, a sense of excitement washed over me. It was astonishing to think that the Angels were genuinely communicating with me through these numbers!

Then, the moment arrived. The senior partner entered the office, and my phone displayed 11:10. He passed my desk and went into his office, followed by the other attorney. Seizing the moment, I hurried after him, eager to escape the confines of the office. Armed with the Angels' confirmation, I knew it was time to leave.

I approached them, stating I needed a moment of their time, emphasizing it would be brief. Directly addressing the tension in the office, I looked at the attorney I had been at odds with and informed him that his comfort in the office would improve without my presence, hence my immediate resignation. Handing over my office and building cards, I turned to leave when the senior partner asked if I could stay to finish the day to assist them. In line with my compassionate nature, I agreed. However, after another twenty minutes, I realized I owed them nothing and left. They were surprised, and the attorney who disliked me seemed relieved, albeit he tried to conceal it. Since then, they have provided me with negative references.

Sharing the news with my daughter only fueled her anger. She accused me of jealousy and imitation, claiming I was encroaching on her aspirations. This accusation drove a deeper wedge between us, exacerbating the distance that had grown over the past three years. She had previously warned me of a day when she would cut off all contact, leaving me with regrets. That day seemed to be approaching faster than we had anticipated.

Regarding my spiritual journey, my daughter claimed credit, but the effort was entirely mine. I started by exploring various Tarot readings, noticing overlapping messages among different readers, which confirmed their authenticity for me. Eventually, I connected with one or two readers whose energy resonated with mine, and I began following their daily readings as part of their collective.

Meditation became a significant part of my routine, with guided meditations from a social media site proving particularly beneficial. These meditations were tailored to specific needs, including integrating the Inner Child with the Higher Self and the Divine. I also explored guided hypnosis and past life regression sessions. These resources offered diverse approaches to connecting with my Inner Child, Higher Self, Christ Self, and the Divine in that specific order. Spending time in quiet meditation or prayer, immersing myself in Mayan tribal music and Celtic flute tunes, engaging in somatic exercises, grounding, and embracing nature all contribute significantly to healing the Inner Child and fostering integration with the Higher Self, Christ Self, and the Divine. Then, I began to listen more intently to my intuition. If an inner voice suggested,

"I should go outside and ground," I followed. If it proposed a visit to the park, I went. And when it prompted meditation, I meditated—sometimes for hours without interruption.

My mornings started at 5:00 a.m. with a walk, followed by a period of sitting and contemplating the Tarot reading for the day. Sometimes, meditation came first; other times, it was continuing a conversation with the Divine that began on my walk, which I recorded on my phone. During moments of doubt and fear, I sought signs from the Divine, finding confirmation in the appearance of a Cardinal, a butterfly, a Blue Jay, a Crow, or two outside my patio door. Although most of my confirmations came from readings, I've been learning to trust my intuition or the sensations arising from shifts in energy.

I discovered that during meditation or prayer and while taking walks in nature, the Divine communicated with me through clear audible messages, visions, thoughts, and internal dialogues—there were many avenues of connection. We all have the capacity to connect with the Divine, beginning with engaging our Inner Child, which initiates the journey towards the Divine.

This path of discovery was one I had to navigate alone. No one guided me on how to begin this magnificent journey towards a life of truth and love—a genuine relationship with the Divine. My experience was not confined to sitting in a building on Sunday mornings, discussing Bible verses in a classroom setting, or attending Sunday services, despite the true Sabbath being

Saturday. I realized I could cultivate a relationship through my Christ consciousness, connecting me to the Divine as Christ intended, without the need for Christian propaganda.

I delved into the practice of setting intentions and manifesting goals, abundance, and material wealth. As my journey deepened, I understood that my focus, and that of the collective, would be more beneficially placed on healing my Inner Child—addressing my traumas and learning self-love—rather than solely on manifesting physical items. I explored the significance of Moon Phases and Angel Numbers, learning about Star seeds, Light workers, Earth Angels, Indigo Children, and the various terms for those deemed "Chosen."

However, the truth is that we all made the conscious decision to exist during this period of linear history. We were aware of the unfolding events in the Age of Aquarius, which is why we are here: to witness, participate, heal our traumas, and integrate our Inner Child Consciousness with our Shadow Self Consciousness and Higher Self Consciousness. This integration aims to connect us to our Christ Consciousness, subsequently to the Collective Christ Consciousness, and finally, to the Divine.

The ultimate goal is to elevate the planet's consciousness to the "Kingdom of Heaven" within us, a connection to the Divine that has existed since before creation. We have been a part of the Divine since before the concept of creation emerged. We are eternities old, sparks of the Divine's light, created in the image of our Higher Self—our Soul, not our human form. As manifesters and creators, we embody aspects of the Divine.

This knowledge is erased from our memory with each reincarnation. Stories, often from children under the age of five, recount their past lives with details that have been verified as accurate. These accounts suggest that the child lived as the person they described in a previous life. In these past lives, roles can fluctuate; a victim and perpetrator might choose to switch roles in subsequent lives, perhaps not through murder but through other karmic circumstances.

Relationships also transform, with spouses potentially becoming parents and children in another life, among various other scenarios. Unfortunately, we don't retain these memories unless we undergo past life regression therapy. Such therapy is said to aid in healing both past life and current traumas. While I haven't personally experienced this type of therapy, I'm deeply fascinated by its potential.

I devoted a significant portion of my time to meditation, engaging in deep conversations with my Higher Self, Ancestors, Spirit Guides, Angels, Ancient Masters, and even the Divine itself. Hours were spent sometimes in tears, trying to understand why I was unable to release the pain and suffering caused by my mother. I pondered why forgiving the man responsible for the mental torment tied to specific memories was easier compared to the traumatic memory of confronting him in her presence— her hysterical screams, the fear of her retaliation, and him, guilt-ridden with his head in his hands. The fear of who would lash out at me first was palpable, as she blamed me, and he was furious for my speaking out. It was then that my Dark Night of the Soul caught up with me—my Tower began to crumble, and I could no longer flee from my emotions; it was time to confront them directly. Aware of forty-six years of suppressed emotions—rage, heartbreak, disappointment, fear—I had disconnected from every negative feeling, pushing it deep down inside. I hadn't anticipated the overwhelming resurgence of these emotions, not trickling in but flooding back all at once. At times, I went through a roll and a half of toilet paper in a single session just from blowing my nose! Hours were spent talking, crying, shouting, swearing, seeking answers, and asking for confirmation of channeled messages.

Progress was being made—significant progress. I began to notice a shift in my demeanor, feeling genuinely positive about the changes within me. I looked forward to my 5:00 a.m. walks, the enlightening conversations with the Divine, and the channeled messages I received. Devoting two to three hours a day to meditation and dialogue with my soul/spirit team, I felt a profound sense of advancement and took pride in my achievements.

Just when I began to make tangible progress and started feeling good about myself, my daughter would inevitably appear, undermining me with her belittling comments. She would dredge up my past negativity as if trying to reattach the burdens I had worked so hard to shed. Despite knowing the effort I was putting in and the significant strides I was making, she chose to tear me down, claiming her status as a Star seed and the "Chosen One" was the reason for my progress. According to her, any positive changes in my life were solely due to her breaking a generational curse, dismissing my efforts entirely. This onslaught crushed my confidence and sense of self-worth, halting my journey for several weeks. I struggled to reengage with my spiritual path with the same heart and commitment as before. Attempting to refocus on my journey proved difficult, as her discouragement had deeply impacted me. I started doubting the authenticity of my experiences, convincing myself that the communications I believed were from the Divine were just figments of my imagination. I felt disconnected, no longer unique to the Divine, and doubted my purpose and the messages I received. It had been weeks since my last walk or meditation session, and my conversations with the Divine had ceased. Her actions not only halted my progress but regressed my healing journey beyond its starting point. I realized the extent of my growth, only for her to undermine it completely, stripping away any pride I had managed to cultivate in myself.

She blamed me for my lack of self-esteem and criticized me for not taking action, yet she failed to recognize that her interventions were the very reason my progress was dismantled. Every attempt at building my self-esteem, confidence, and worth was met with her resistance. And whenever I tried to establish boundaries, she accused me of being selfish and gaslighting. Her presence and actions became significant barriers to my healing and growth, leaving me silenced and unable to advocate for myself in the face of her continuous disparagement.

I received a reading that was incredibly encouraging, highlighting the great strides I had made and cautioning me not to let anyone derail my journey. The message suggested that there were individuals who wished for my failure, actively hindering my progress. This message felt uniquely intended for me, reigniting my dedication to my path of healing. I delved even more profoundly, dedicating up to eight hours a day to meditation. I shifted my listening habits away from mainstream music to focus exclusively on meditation and frequency music, especially while driving. This isn't the kind of music that induces sleep but instead tunes that resonate with the Divine frequency or grounding vibrations. They help me stay relaxed and address my road rage issues, fostering a more peaceful and loving mindset towards myself and others. Yes, we are always in progress, learning to love ourselves and extend that love to others.

The moral teaching of loving our neighbor as we love ourselves is one I've heard since childhood. As I learn to love myself, empathy flows abundantly from me. However, finding grace, mercy, and love for others can be challenging due to the widespread presence of child abuse, pedophilia, neglect, animal cruelty, domestic violence, violence against women, elder abuse, world hunger, crime, overdoses, sex trafficking, and homelessness.

These are issues that the wealthy could address immediately if they chose to, which is why it's difficult for me to fully embrace love for my fellow human beings. I see those with the means to improve the world but choose self-interest over communal well-being as particularly harmful – sometimes even worthless.

I wish no harm upon anyone, but I recognize that Karma is a force that ensures everyone faces the consequences of their actions, completing their Karmic Cycle eventually. In this Age of Aquarius, it seems these reckonings will come sooner rather than later.

I had been focusing on setting my intentions to manifest various goals: securing a job, paying off my house by the end of 2023, paying off my car by the same year, and meeting my Soulmate during the Full Moon in August 2023. With my finances dwindling and the need for employment becoming urgent, I yearned for a change. After nearly forty years of work, I felt weary; at sixty-one, I believed I had dedicated enough of my life to labor. Despite uncertainties about how to achieve it, as a creator and more manifest with the support of the Divine and my spirit team, I decided to pursue retirement.

While grounding under the sun on the day of the Full Moon, I queried the Divine about altering my previously set intentions. The affirmative response from the Divine was encouraging: "Yes, you can – go ahead, say what you want – visualize it – feel it - make it happen." Envisioning my desires, I saw them vividly— every color, detail, and aspect of the life I wanted, including my Soulmate (though his face remained unclear). A warm sensation filled my body, and my Third Eye Chakra brightened, indicating a miraculous occurrence. It was clear that the Divine was working through me, facilitating a moment of true manifestation.

During the next New Moon, a time for releasing undesired elements and setting intentions for upcoming manifestations, I performed a Salt Bath Cleanse. This ritual was meant to purge negative energy and outline my desires: rebirth as a child of the Universe, a fresh start, a new life, encountering my Soulmate and Soul tribe, achieving financial security upon retirement, and settling all outstanding debts by year's end. However, in setting these intentions and manifesting them, I overlooked the importance of precision in my desires. It's crucial to be mindful of what you manifest, as the universe takes your words, thoughts, and requests seriously. The unfolding events tested my faith, revealing the Divine's presence and affirming my role as the Magician of the Tarot, equipped with all necessary tools for manifestation.

Being raised Catholic, I was taught that the only way to have a personal relationship with the Divine was through Christ the Son. According to this belief, the path to the Divine is exclusively through Christ. The priest serves as Christ's representative on Earth, suggesting that one must go through Christ to reach the Divine, with a hierarchy that extends from Senior Priest to Deacon to Bishop and finally to the Pope, who is viewed as God's representation on Earth. I was baptized as an infant to cleanse me of the Original Sin committed by Adam and Eve, but this act did not guarantee a place in Heaven, nor did it absolve me of all sins despite being "washed in the Blood of Jesus Christ" who died for humanity's sins.

Later, in my 30s, the Free Methodist Church (with similar beliefs to the Baptists) introduced me to the concept of a personal relationship with Christ, yet still within the framework of Christian doctrine. Access to the Divine (God the Father) was still mediated by Christ. To have a relationship with Christ and, subsequently, with the Divine, one had to be baptized and cleansed of sin in Christ's name, signifying a rebirth that purportedly ensured a place in Heaven by forgiving all past, present, and future sins due to Christ's sacrifice.

However, a Spiritual Awakening Journey diverges from this path—it involves a profound, introspective examination of the Inner Self, confronting deep and often dark truths about oneself, known as "Shadow Work." This journey also enlightens one about the behaviors of others and their reactions and approaches toward you. Patterns in both oneself and others become evident, and you begin to recognize who the Divine is distancing you from as you discover your true Inner Self, heal your Inner Child, and address your trauma—a universal experience we all share.

You will start to hear your intuition (Higher Self) guide you in situations, discerning people's energies, making decisions, and learning to trust every "gut" feeling. This intuition eventually becomes instinctive, strengthening your bond with your Spirit Team (Higher Self, Guardian Angels, Spirit Guides, Ancestors, and Ancient Masters), which in turn deepens your connection to your Christ Consciousness and directly to the Divine. This connection to your Christ Consciousness and the Divine has always been present, affirming that we are, and have always been, directly connected to the Divine as it was intended.Not long after the Full Moon, my life began to shift, becoming strained and spiraling out of control. At the time, I didn't realize I had initiated this turmoil myself, marking the peak of my Dark Night of the Soul. Circumstances started to unfold: by September 2023, I had made the last mortgage payment my bank account could cover. The car payment due at month's end loomed over me.

Since July, I had been relying on credit cards to manage monthly expenses, including phone and household bills, which were now maxed out. Financially, things were becoming dire, and I found myself in a predicament I hadn't faced since my late 20s. My faith was waning as I questioned why the Divine seemed to have forsaken me. Every job interview led nowhere, bills accumulated, groceries ran low, I was short on medication, the cats needed food and litter, and even toilet paper became a concern. Panic set in.

Meanwhile, my Tarot readings offered reassurance that abundance was on its way, urging me to "keep the faith" and promising that my manifestations and wish fulfillments were imminent. They indicated that things were shifting in my favor and that the challenges I faced were not obstacles but opportunities for renewal, clearing out the old to welcome the new.

Yet, amidst the chaos, I couldn't see past my immediate fears about the future—how to secure funds without employment, how to survive. Consumed by worry, I once again neglected my spiritual practices. In desperation, I turned to the internet seeking quick financial solutions, devoted time to writing a book, and applied for state assistance, rationalizing that after contributing to tax funds for over thirty-five years and supporting others in their times of need, it was now my turn to seek help.

I had noticed numerous advertisements for selling homes "as is" for cash. Financially constrained and facing challenges in finding employment, I remembered how my last employer gave a negative reference for a former secretary, leading me to suspect that I wouldn't receive a favorable reference either, given my abrupt departure. Through spiritually channeled messages and meditation, I came to understand that my missed job opportunities were aligned with my desire to retire by the end of 2023 and be financially secure. Indeed, I retired at the end of the year with sufficient funds to sustain myself.

Faced with the imminent need for income to cover my house payments and with no other options in sight, I reached out to a "buy your home for cash now" company for an estimate. After submitting a video showcasing my home's interior and exterior, they scheduled an in-person visit the following day, and by that afternoon, I received a proposal. Seeking assurance, I requested a second opinion and received a similar offer. Reluctantly, I decided to sell my home, as it was my last resort for financial liquidity. The suspension of credit card payments and the cancellation of my daughter and granddaughter's car insurance and phone service were further measures I took to reduce expenses, which only added strain to my relationship with my daughter.

The house was listed on October 1st, sold by October 16th, and the closing occurred on November 17th. By October 27th, I had vacated the premises. Packing a three-bedroom house on my own was a monumental task. I hired two men and a truck for the move, but some items went missing since I couldn't supervise them constantly by myself.

The moving expenses exceeded my budget, and I resorted to using credit cards to cover the costs. Additionally, I borrowed money from a gentleman who had been voluntarily mowing my lawn since June after we became friends through a neighborhood app where I had sought lawn care assistance. Our relationship was platonic, occasionally sharing meals, but it did not develop beyond friendship. After repaying him and the passing of Christmas, our communication ceased. With the proceeds from selling my home, I calculated that I would have enough to cover a year's rent and continue my car payments until I could secure employment or devise a new plan for my future. I was receiving EBT benefits and had state-aided medical insurance for medical care, which helped reduce my expenses significantly, including a reduced phone bill and car insurance. However, I was unable to make payments on my credit cards. Three months into this situation, my credit score had plummeted from 760 to below 400, and I was aware of the potential legal actions creditors could take if I failed to pay. Yet, I remained hopeful that I would secure funds before facing any lawsuits.

The year 2023 was concluding as the most challenging year of my life. I had worked diligently to achieve what I had—my house, a reliable car, and sufficient funds to cover my bills with some to spare. I found myself questioning everything: What went wrong? Why did I lose everything? Had I been forsaken? Did I deserve this fate? I even pondered if my daughter's claims held any truth—was she indeed dispensing Karma as a Star seed endowed with such power by the Divine, or was I just being paranoid?

As my world seemed to collapse, thoughts of ending my life began to surface, especially during drives home from unsuccessful job interviews, knowing I had botched them and it would be weeks before another opportunity arose. I was running out of time, desperately pleading with the Divine, contemplating if suicide might be the answer to end my financial struggles and bring peace—a state I had longed for but never experienced. The idea of peace sounded incredibly enticing, in stark contrast to my spiraling despair. This period felt like either a profound Dark Night of the Soul or as if someone was casting spells or curses against me.

On the day I closed on the house, I woke to find my oldest cat severely ill. As he lay on the wooden floors, he constantly shifted from side to side, seeking comfort. His gentle steps seemed painful, as if bearing his weight was a struggle. This had been his condition for the three weeks we spent in our new residence, worsening over three years of illness.

Despite my sporadic attempts at medicating him, his doctor had informed me that his condition was irreversible. His thyroid disease caused incessant hunger, leading him to consume not only his food but any leftovers from my other cat and any food I or visitors had. It was a relentless symptom of his ailment, and witnessing his suffering over the last three years was heart-wrenching.

In his final six weeks, he lost the ability to jump onto the bed, having lost all muscle mass, and in his last week, he couldn't even reach the recliner. It was devastating to see him in such a state. Thus, that morning, I made the difficult decision to say goodbye. Hours later, still engulfed in sorrow, I signed the closing papers for the house. The following weeks were some of the darkest of my life, with a lonely Thanksgiving and a joyless Christmas.

The image of him lying lifeless haunted me, alongside a deep sense of guilt for possibly acting too hastily in ending his suffering. On our way to the vet, he cried just once, a departure from his usual loud protests when confined. It seemed as if he knew what was to come, either resigned to his fate or too weak to resist. Perhaps that's just my projection, but I still grapple with guilt, questioning if I let him go too soon despite a nagging feeling that his suffering had become unbearable. His demeanor was always somber, contradicting his healthy blood tests, leading me to believe he was deeply unhappy. It's said that pets mirror their owners' personalities, and perhaps his final days spent in the bathroom were his way of signaling his time was near—a behavior I've come to associate with a cat's impending death. Throughout his last years, he communicated incessantly, meowing as if trying to tell me something, likely expressing his constant hunger. Now, I find myself missing those meows more than I ever thought possible, a testament to the bond we shared.

Before he passed, he lost his voice. Even when he was healthy, his meows were quiet, but he used to at least emit a loud purring sound when exhaling. Near the end, that sound vanished, regardless of his efforts to meow or push air through. He appeared to struggle just to keep his head up, and his exhaustion was evident in his eyes. Every morning, like clockwork, he vomited for months until one day, he made a guttural noise as though expelling his insides, and then the morning sickness ceased abruptly.

After that, his behavior changed: he moved slower rested on the floor more, yet his appetite remained unchanged, and he drank a lot of water, which wasn't out of the ordinary for him. Despite these signs, all his medical tests returned normal except for his thyroid condition. This situation persisted for a long time. I was reluctant to let him go; he was my constant, the one aspect of my life that never failed me, remaining steadfast through my toughest times.

The decision to say goodbye was excruciating. Even in his frailty, he resisted my attempts to cuddle, visibly exhausted and seemingly aware that his time had come. Letting him go felt like closing a chapter of my own life in 2023, laying to rest a part of my former self. I still find myself on the verge of tears when I think of him, but I often halt my grief, punishing myself as if I don't have the right to mourn him due to my failure to adequately address his illness. This behavior reflects a darker aspect of myself that I need to confront—why I sometimes neglected his needs yet at other times provided for him unconditionally. This pattern mirrored my parenting approach with my children, oscillating between nurture and insisting they toughen up. It reminds me of my mother's contradictory actions: offering comfort only to take it away with the next breath.

After the turmoil subsided and I had the chance to reflect on the events, it became clear that the sequence of losses—my home, the potential loss of my car, my children, and my beloved pet of 17 years—was, in fact, manifestations of everything I had set in my intentions, serving as a cleansing of all that no longer served my highest good. During the New Moon and in that Salt Bath, I had sought a new beginning, a clean slate, a new life, a rebirth, and retirement by the end of 2023.

Remarkably, by year's end, each of these desires had materialized in ways I hadn't anticipated. The realization struck me profoundly; a true "light bulb moment," acknowledging the comprehensive removal of everyone and everything from my life, was precisely what I had asked for.

The unfolding of events began to make sense. To retire and achieve financial security, all my expenses needed to be eliminated. The house, being paid off, was no longer a financial burden, although I hadn't specified retaining ownership in my manifestation intentions.

This experience taught me the importance of precise wording in setting intentions for manifestation. I've been honing the skill of monitoring my thoughts, striving to reframe them positively. However, I recently encountered a perspective that mere positive thinking is insufficient for personal or collective transformation.

Instead, it's about utilizing the faint illumination from our past—the light revealing our Shadow Self, akin to a shadow cast in front of us—to focus on what requires healing within our Inner Child and trauma. It's essential to delve into the past to heal our Inner Child's trauma and integrate with our Higher Self, thereby aligning with the present and paving the way for our future. This approach resonates deeply with me, offering a clear path forward.Since June 2023 and into the early months of 2024, I've been receiving messages that elucidate the progress of my journey, including my transition, transcendence, integration, and healing. These communications have shed light on my mother's behaviors, reactions, and responses, as well as the dynamics between my parents' irresponsible, misogynistic, and narcissistic actions.

They've also touched upon how my own actions contributed to my children's decision to cut contact with me, the potential feelings of regret, guilt, and shame my mother might harbor in my absence, and my own feelings of regret, guilt, and shame due to the estrangement from my children. Additionally, I've gained insights into various aspects of my Shadow Self and discovered how self-talk therapy has significantly aided in healing my Inner Child. Listening to recordings of my progress, I'm amazed by how far I've come. Moreover, my relationship with the Divine has deepened, offering a newfound understanding free from external prescriptions on how this connection should be felt, expressed, or navigated, provided it respects legal and personal boundaries and adheres to moral and legal standards.

This period of isolation has transformed me in profound ways, leaving me feeling like an entirely different person from who I was just last week, let alone last year. I take pride in the person I've evolved into but struggle with missing those the Divine has removed from my life. I'm learning to accept that if they were meant to remain, the Divine would not have taken them away, trusting that if it's meant to be, they'll return in Divine timing.

Since October 2023, there's been no contact, and the ease with which one can be forgotten, especially as a parent, is challenging to come to terms with. It underscores the regrets and mistakes parents grow to recognize, often too late to correct. Despite the expectation that I would have moved on by now, the pain persists. Raised with the belief in loving our enemies and praying for those who sin against us, I also acknowledge the inevitability of Karma, understanding that cycles must be completed regardless of prayer.

Thus, I'm torn between loving them, praying for them, or attempting to erase them from memory, as they seem to have done with me. At times, it's unclear whether their absence is a result of their own Karmic debts or if I am still navigating my own Karmic Cycle. Yet, I believe I have resolved the Karma accrued in this lifetime and in past lives, having fulfilled the necessary cycles.

I've come to understand that my Karmic Cycle has closed its loop. My mother emotionally neglected, abandoned, and physically abused me—a pattern I unfortunately repeated with my daughter through emotional and physical abuse (and, according to his father, abandonment) toward my son. In a reflection of the pain my mother caused me, I chose a stance of no contact as punishment; similarly, my daughter uses her critical view of me as her form of retribution, echoing my mother's abusive tendencies. My children's absence from my life, motivated by their feelings towards me, completes this cycle— my personal generational trauma manifesting through both this lifetime and past ones.

This realization dawned on me after losing everything, highlighting that I still occasionally wrestle with negative thoughts about myself, my future, and my manifestations. My soul's awakening journey, aimed at connecting with the Collective and drawing us closer to the Divine, is ongoing. My purpose will persist until my final breath in this incarnation as my Higher Self navigates this plane of existence. This journey allows the Divine to explore every conceivable emotion and life experience.

It's said that the lifetime in which you undergo your Spiritual Awakening marks your last earthly incarnation. After living thousands of lives, experiencing a spiritual awakening signifies knowing your true self, learning all intended lessons, completing your Karmic Cycle, and fulfilling your purpose, allowing you to finally "go home" without the necessity of returning. I eagerly anticipate this truth, hoping to return to the Divine, to reunite with my purest form—"light," and achieve Nirvana.

This revelation filled me with excitement, motivating me to embark on my journey and fulfill my purpose. Even if the process spans another forty years, I am reassured by the knowledge that upon completing my earthly duties, I will return to the Creator, to the essence of all existence, to what has always been. This universal truth, despite varying names and understandings of the system, is perhaps the one consensus everyone seems to reach.

Now that I've settled into my new home and am welcoming the New Year, I've made every effort to create a cozy and welcoming space. Although I don't have many of my personal items around due to limited space, I trust that the Divine has placed me exactly where I need to be. The year is 2024, an even number, which breaks down to 8 (2+2+4=8)—a figure associated with abundance and good fortune in Angel Number symbolism. Interestingly, my new address is 512 (5+1+2=8), resonating with Angel Number 8.

Numerous readings have indicated that this year is destined for abundance and good fortune, not just for me but for the collective as well. Moreover, we are entering the Age of Aquarius, a time characterized by discovery, the unveiling of secrets, and the commencement of Karma cycles for many, both positive and negative.

In this Age of Aquarius, it is believed that whatever Karma that has been accumulated throughout this lifetime—and presumably past lifetimes—will come to fruition. This period marks a time when the world's secrets are being revealed, the truth uncovered, and individuals begin facing the consequences of their actions. My journey thus far has been about overcoming the trauma bond that battered my Inner Child, shattered my

Higher Self, and crippled me as a person. This has been the longest and hardest battle of my life, spanning 46 years, largely as a silent tormentor. The process brought everything into the open, exposing the truth—that the trauma wasn't mine to bear. It was my mother's trauma, her grief, and her rage, all unfairly laid upon me.

I began to see the reasons behind our actions and feelings. The Divine illuminated everything, allowing me to understand, to see the truth of our existences—my mother's malice, my father's cruelty, and the darkness within myself. These revelations represented the Karmic debt I had accumulated over many lifetimes, which I finally settled in 2023. I atoned for every sin committed, paving the way for the greatest gift: my abundance, my new beginning, as promised by the Divine. This is the dawn of that new chapter. It's a time to let go of everything that no longer serves my highest good, deepen my connection with the divine, embrace nature, and remember that everything unfolds with divine purpose and timing. The Divine's call can come at the most unexpected moments, especially when life seems to be unraveling. When you find yourself questioning your path, feeling lost and desperate for guidance—this is your Higher Self, pushing you towards your Spiritual Awakening Journey.

It's a sign that you're facing your Dark Night of the Soul, a pivotal moment when the Divine is calling you to connect with your Christ consciousness. This is the beginning of the most crucial journey you will ever undertake, the one leading you home.

Answer the call!

Shout for joy to the Lord, all the earth. Worship the Lord with gladness; come before him with joyful songs. Know that the Lord is God. It is he who made us, and we are his; we are his people, the sheep of his pasture. Enter his gates with thanksgiving and his courts with praise; give thanks to him and praise his name. For the Lord is good and his love endures forever; his faithfulness continues through all generations.

—Psalm 100

* 9 7 9 8 2 2 7 9 4 7 4 9 9 *